GROUNDED:
Anchoring the Evangelical Sermon in Theological Doctrine

David W. Brown

Grounded: *Anchoring the Evangelical Sermon in Theological Doctrine*

Published by JEM Group, Inc.
Atlanta, GA
Copyright © 2014 by David W. Brown

International Standard Book Number: 978-0-9816582-2-3
Library of Congress Control Number: 2014930397
Printed in the United States of America

ALL RIGHTS RESERVED

Neither this book nor any part may be reproduced or transmitted in any form or by any means, electronic or mechanical, including photocopying, microfilming, and recording, or by any information storage and retrieval system, without permission in writing from the author.

For Information:

JEM Group, Inc.
Atlanta, GA
www.morris-group.com

To Melinda, for your continued love, support, and patience

CONTENTS

ACKNOWLEDGEMENTS...iii

INTRODUCTION
Drifting Away from Theological Doctrine..................................1
Drifting Away from Theologically Based Study............................3
Reclaiming Evangelical Orthodoxy in the Pulpit 3
The Purpose of the Book 4

CHAPTERS/BODY
Sermons about Faith and Discipleship
1. Hebrews 5:11- 6:12 Commentary and Interpretation......................9
   Sermon Outline: Growing Up or Growing Old: The Life Long Process of Spiritual Maturity...14
2. Colossians 1:3-14 Commentary and Interpretation......................19
   Sermon Outline: Thanksgiving and Christian Living: Giving Thanks to the Father for the Work He has Accomplished through His Son 24
3. Philippians 2:1-11 Commentary and Interpretation.....................29
   Sermon Outline: WWJT - What Would Jesus Think? Godly Thinking that Leads to Godly Living.......................................34
4. Mark 4:35-41 Commentary and Interpretation 39
   Sermon Outline: Building Faith through the Storms of Life: Stories of Faith in Mark's Gospel..43
5. Matthew 26:36-56 Commentary and Interpretation 47
   Sermon Outline: Trial, Prayer, and Submission: Learning to Overcome Trials through Prayer and Submission...............................52

Sermons that use Parables
6. Luke 11:1-13 Commentary and Interpretation...........................59
   Sermon Outline: Prayers, Midnight Travelers, and Good Gifts: Luke's Parable about the Gift of Prayer 63
7. Luke 15:11-32 Commentary and Interpretation..........................67
   Sermon Outline: Lost Sheep, Lost Coins, and Lost Sons: Three Parables Pointing to One Savior and His Work................................72
8. Mark 4:3-25 Commentary and Interpretation 77
   Sermon Outline: True Discipleship and Israel's Failure to Listen: Mark's Parable of the Soils 82
9. Matthew 25:1-13 Commentary and Interpretation 87
   Sermon Outline: Parable, Metaphor, and Readiness: Are we Prepared for the Coming of our Lord? 92
10. Matthew 25:14-30 Commentary and Interpretation 97
    Sermon Outline: Money, Stewardship and the Second Coming of Christ: Evaluating our Readiness in Light of the Coming of our Lord 102

Sermons about Character Formation

11. Matthew 7:13-29 Commentary and Interpretation 109
    Sermon Outline: Two Gates, Two Trees, and Two Houses: Pairing up to Make a Point about Character Formation 114
12. Ecclesiastes 1:1-11 Commentary and Interpretation 119
    Sermon Outline: The Futility of Mankind's Endeavor without God: Life without God amounts to Nothing 124
13. James 3:1-18 Commentary and Interpretation. 129
    Sermon Outline: Taming the Tongue: Using Metaphor and Wisdom to Shape the Character of the Believer. 133

Sermons that use the Psalter

14. Psalm 1:1-6 Commentary and Interpretation 139
    Sermon Outline: Torah, Metaphor, and Simile: Using Literary Devices to Describe Two Paths in Life 144
15. Psalm 19:1-14 Commentary and Interpretation 149
    Sermon Outline: Moving from the Sun to the Law: A Psalm of Metaphor and Illumination 154
16. Psalm 23:1-6 Commentary and Interpretation 159
    Sermon Outline: The Lord as Shepherd and Host: Looking to God as our Protector, Guide, and Restorer. 164
17. Psalm 42:1- 43:5 Commentary and Interpretation. 169
    Sermon Outline: Moving from Despair to Restoration: A Psalm for the Frail and the Homebound 174
18. Psalm 115:1-18 Commentary and Interpretation. 179
    Sermon Outline: Trusting God to Shape Believers into His Divine Image: A Psalm of Trust. 184

Sermons about the Temple and Worship

19. Ezekiel 43:1-9 Commentary and Interpretation. 191
    Sermon Outline: New Temples, Sacred Spaces and the Presence of God: Preparations and Declarations for Worship 196
20. John 4:7-26 Commentary and Interpretation 201
    Sermon Outline: Temples, Outcasts, and Worship: Moving from the Temple of God to God as the Temple. 205

CONCLUSION 211

BIBLIOGRAPHY 215

ACKNOWLEDGEMENTS

I am greatly indebted to a number of people without whom this project would not have taken place. I am deeply thankful to Laura Jesseph and Emma Morris for their efforts in various areas that ranged from grammar to proof reading, to publication. Their warmth and their friendship were only surpassed by their tireless efforts. I am also indebted to Megan Lynch who worked tirelessly with me at editing and proofing this text. Meg was a walking goldmine of grammatical expertise and patience. Her friendship, efforts, and expertise were enormously helpful in the successful completion of this project.

I am also grateful to Shawn Parker, and John Morris for their gracious endorsements that appear on the back cover. Despite their busy schedules each one took time out of their day to read excerpts from the book and write an endorsement. I am deeply appreciative for their efforts and friendships. In addition, John also proofed the book and offered a number of suggestions that ranged from grammar to format, to theology. His insight and friendship are forever appreciated. I also must thank my wife Melinda who continued to encourage me despite her numerous health issues. She has become a model of Christian love and perseverance for me.

Finally, my greatest appreciation goes to my Lord Jesus, who took an ignorant and arrogant man, and educated and humbled him. To Him, I give my all.

David Brown
Summer 2013

INTRODUCTION

Drifting Away from Theological Doctrine

As a preacher, I am often asked how long it takes me to write a sermon. The answer may surprise you. I usually spend between seven and ten hours preparing and writing a sermon. Sound expository sermons take an enormous amount of time to create.

The great American inventor Thomas Edison once said, "Opportunity is missed by most people because it is dressed in overalls and looks like hard work."[i] The same idea holds true for sermon preparation as well because great sermons rarely come about at the exact moment the preacher sits down to write. Great sermons are developed over time and typically progress in stages as the pastor regularly revisits, edits, and improves the sermon. Great sermons take hard work, enormous study, and a pastor who is keenly aware of the direction of God's spirit during his/her study time. Great sermons come about from a proper orthodox understanding of Scripture and basic application of sound principles for interpretation.

Unfortunately, in this age of technology, the sermon message has sometimes been eclipsed by electronic snippets and PowerPoint presentations in an effort to hold the congregation's attention. While technology has its advantages, what are needed in evangelical pulpits are sermons that not only teach solid theological doctrine of the Christian faith, but also bridge the gap between biblical interpretation and sermon proclamation.

Today, studies on the internal life of the church show that evangelicals are becoming increasingly illiterate from a biblical perspective.[ii] We are coming to know less and less about our Bible and Christian doctrine as time goes by. According to David Wells, the situation has reached a crisis as the church has drifted away from its First Love and focused on

Introduction

increasing church attendance at the peril of sound theology. Wells rightly laments:

> *Where this modern "wisdom" comes to supplant confession in defining and disciplining what practice should mean, where reflection has been reduced simply to reflection upon the self, and where the hard work of relating the truth of God's Word to the processes of modern life has been abandoned, there once again theology has died, and all that is left of it is an empty shell of what wisdom used to be.* [iii]

As a result, many evangelicals, myself included, feel that we are moving away from solid theological teaching of the Scriptures in our churches.[iv] The need for sound theological teaching from the pulpit has never been greater than today. Recent publication of books by so-called evangelical pastors who claim the Gospel message has been hijacked[v] serve only to emphasize the need for theologically-based sermons.

Despite the existing problems, our generation is not unique to these circumstances.[vi] Martin Luther lamented about the same situation in his day. After visiting parishes in the fall of 1528, Luther decided something had to be done. He wrote:

> *The deplorable conditions which I recently encountered when I was a visitor constrained me to prepare this brief and simple catechism or statement of Christian teaching. Good God, what wretchedness I beheld! The common people, especially those who live in the country, have no knowledge whatever of Christian teaching, and unfortunately many pastors are quite incompetent and unfitted for teaching. Although the people are supposed to be Christian, are baptized, and receive the holy sacraments, they do not know the Lord's prayer, the creed, or the ten commandments; they live as if they were pigs and irrational beasts, and now that the Gospel has been restored, they have mastered the fine art of abusing liberty.*[vii]

There is growing evidence by Christian scholars that reflects the lack of theological education and its practice to be the root cause as to why many evangelical Christians have failed to grow to full spiritual maturity.[viii] This fundamental failure of educational and spiritual discipline has even

Introduction

affected the way we study our Bibles. For example, chapter divisions, at times, fall in the middle of biblical passages, and this can lead the reader astray from the true meaning portrayed in the passage read.

Drifting Away from Theologically Based Study

With the invention of the printing press in the middle of the fifteenth century, there was a shift from handwritten manuscripts to printed Bibles. While the advancement of this great technological breakthrough heralded the mass production of books, it also brought about a decline in the use of the mind. Christians in the past had memorized stories and large portions of the Bible.[ix] However, following the advent of the printing press, believers came to memorize substantially smaller literary units called verse numbers.

In 1551, the Stephanus edition of the Greek New Testament was published in Paris. The edition is noteworthy, since Stephanus included chapter divisions and verse numbers for the first time, and this led to the publication of the Geneva Bible in 1560.[x] This Bible was the first English Bible to be published with chapter divisions and verse numbers.[xi] While this handy new tool was extremely useful in locating passages, what emerged over time was exegesis that was derived from these location tools rather than existing literary narrative devices within the text.[xii] As Bibles with chapter divisions and verse numbers became increasingly more popular through numerous publications, reading the Bible as a story faded into oblivion.[xiii] Over the course of time, verse number exegesis combined with poor interpretational skills soon eclipsed the former literary narrative methodologies used in the past for biblical interpretation, and this downward spiral greatly impacted sermon preparation in a negative way.[xiv]

Reclaiming Evangelical Orthodoxy in the Pulpit

How do evangelical pastors reclaim that which has been lost? First, there is no substitute for theological study. Pastors must be properly

Introduction

trained in order to prepare sound theological sermons. Seminaries and Bible colleges offer classes on every aspect of theological training, and some of their courses can be taken over the Internet.

In addition, pastors must devote themselves once again to the theological study of God's word and to the development and writing of expository sermons. Evangelical pastors do not have the luxury of standing by while congregations seek services that entertain them or offer self-help remedies to the maladies of life. We must do more than simply play stage tricks with the doctrines of life and death.[xv] When we stand in the pulpit, we must be prepared to deliver a sermon we have studied, practiced, and prayed over.

Finally, since a passage can be located only by identifying the boundaries of the context, verse number exegesis often works contrary to proper interpretation. Pastors must learn and use narrative and contextual methodologies for interpretation and sermon preparation, rather than pulling mistaken meaning through verse number exegesis. Therefore, the pastor/teacher must come to recognize that proper interpretation is found in the context of a passage.

Just as Luther worked to change the setting in his generation, we must also work to overcome the shortcomings of our generation. With the help of our Lord, the hard work of theological study, and dedication to preparing sermons that teach solid theological doctrine, this setting can be overcome once again, even as it was overcome in Luther's day.

The Purpose of the Book

Grounded: Anchoring the Evangelical Sermon in Theological Doctrine has a three-fold purpose. First, the book is to be used as a step-by-step guide for the preacher and Bible teacher to aid in his/her exegesis through various passages of the Bible.[xvi] Proper interpretations will be built upon the Scripture through historical, literary, and grammatical methodologies that will be employed to bring the reader to a solid theological understanding of a given passage that will enable the reader to produce sound theological sermons.

Second, following the hermeneutical section of each chapter will be a homiletical section where a sermon outline for the passage will be given. Building on the ideas gleaned from the hermeneutical section, this book will then step the preacher through the construction of a sermon outline based upon the interpretation of the passage. In fusing together hermeneutics and homiletics, the book will advocate both a proper understanding of the Scripture and the sound methodology used in expository preaching.[xvii]

Building a proper understanding of the Scriptures is only the beginning. *Grounded* will aid preachers and Bible teachers in learning how to identify starting and stopping points in a biblical passage, as well as building sermons and teaching outlines to preach and teach the church. From the introduction of the sermon to the summation, the preacher's goal is to captivate the hearts and minds of the congregation, so that once the sermon is delivered, the hearer would leave the church with a solid understanding of that particular passage and how it applies to his/her life.

Finally, through the use of endnotes and a bibliography at the back of the book, several titles are listed that will aid the education of pastors and Bible teachers in their studies. My hope and prayer is that in the following pages, this book will both aid and educate pastors and Bible students alike in the interpretation and construction of a sermon outline of God's word. In doing so, God's servants can begin to appreciate that great sermons are not thrown together haphazardly, but come about through the hard work of theological study and its application into a sermonic form.

---

[i] Elizabeth Dole, *Hearts Touched with Fire: My 500 Favorite Inspirational Quotations*, (New York: Carroll & Graff Publishers, 2004), 107.

[ii] http://www.barna.org/barna-update/article/12-faithspirituality/325-barna-studies-the-research-offers-a-year-in-review-perspective. For more studies see www.barna.org.

[iii] David Wells, *No Place for Truth or Whatever Happened to Evangelical Theology*, (Grand Rapids: Eerdmans Publishing Company, 1993), 101.

[iv] J.I. Packer, Gary A. Parrett, *Grounded in the Gospel: Building Believers the Old-Fashioned Way*, (Grand Rapids: Baker Books Publishing, 2010). See also Kevin J. Vanhoozer, *The Drama of Doctrine: A Canonical Linguistic Approach to Christian Doctrine*, (Louisville: Westminster John Knox Publishing, 2005).

Introduction

[v] Rob Bell, *Love Wins: A Book About Heaven, Hell, And The Fate of Every Person Who Ever Lived*, (New York: Harper Collins Publishers, 2011). In his preface Bell claimed, "Jesus' story has been hijacked by other stories, stories Jesus wasn't interested in telling, because they have nothing to do with what he came to do." Bell's comment emphasizes my point that some pastors not only misunderstand the stories in the Gospel accounts, but also fail to recognize that the stories themselves were organized in a particular format that highlights the Christian message.

[vi] J. Gresham Machen, *The Minister and His Greek Testament*, in the Orthodox Presbyterian Church, 1918. This article notes the same problem existed in Machen's day as well.

[vii] Martin Luther, *Luther's Small Catechism with Explanation*, (St. Louis: Concordia Publishing House, 2005), 246-47.

[viii] Packer and Parrett, *Ground in the Gospel*, 9.

[ix] Richard Baukham, *Jesus and the Eye Witnesses: The Gospels as Eyewitness Testimonies* (Grand Rapids: William B. Eerdmans Publishing, 2006), 264-89. See also Alan Millard, *Reading and Writing in the Time of Jesus*, (New York: New York University Press, 2000), 154-184. Rosalind Thomas, *Literacy and Orality in Ancient Greece*, (Cambridge: Cambridge University Press, 1992).

[x] Donald L. Brake, *A Visual History of the English Bible: The Tumultuous Tale of the World's Bestselling Book*, (Grand Rapids: Baker Books Publishing, 2008), 233.

[xi] Bruce M. Metzger, *Manuscripts of the Greek Bible: An Introduction to Greek Paleography*, (Oxford: Oxford University Press, 1981), 42.

[xii] Mark A. Knoll, *The Scandal of the Evangelical Mind* (Grand Rapids: William B. Eerdmans Publishing, 1994), 134-35. Knoll refers to this process as the "versification of Scripture."

[xiii] David Rhoads, Joanna Dewey, Donald Michie, "*Mark as Story: An Introduction to the Narrative of a Gospel*" 2nd ed. (Minneapolis, MN, Augsburg Fortress, 1999).

[xiv] Grant R. Osborne, *The Hermeneutical Spiral: A Comprehensive Introduction to Biblical Interpretation* revised and expanded edition (Downers Grove: IVP Press, 2006), 29-30. Osborne makes the connection that poor interpretation has had upon sermon exposition in the church.

[xv] John Ruskin, *Unto This Last and Other Writings*, (London: Penguin Books Publishing, 1985), 266.

[xvi] For reference, I will be using the NASB version of the Bible.

[xvii] Sidney Greidanus, *The Modern Preacher and the Ancient Text: Interpreting and Preaching Biblical Literature* (Grand Rapids: William B. Eerdmans Publishing, 1988) 10-15. Greidanus argued that preaching with the authority of Scripture is synonymous with expository preaching.

Sermons about Faith and Discipleship

David W. Brown

Chapter 1

Hebrews 5:11 - 6:12
Commentary and Interpretation

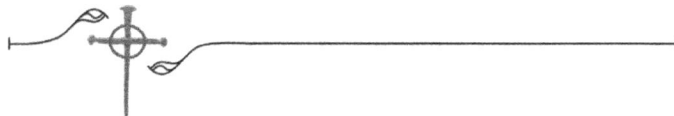

Great sermons encourage believers to grow to spiritual maturity and instruct believers in how to listen to God. Since Bible study is the primary way for believers to hear God, teaching them how to understand and grasp God's word is of utmost importance.

One of the most important parts to preparing a great sermon is recognizing where a passage begins and ends. What would happen if a pastor stood in the pulpit one Sunday morning and began to tell a story, but stopped in the middle of that story? Or contrarily, what if he began in the middle of the story, and the congregation had no idea what he was talking about? This is a classic example of what can happen when we allow chapter divisions and verse numbers to dictate the beginning and ending points of a sermon passage.

Ancient Bibles did not contain chapter divisions and verse numbers as we know them today. These modern location tools were not added into Bibles until the middle of the sixteenth century, shortly after the advent of the printing press.[i] Unfortunately, when these location tools were added, the editors placed a chapter division in the middle of this passage in Hebrews. If we read our Bible from chapter to chapter, as many modern Christians do, we will miss the point of what the author of Hebrews was making in this passage.

This passage is important for a number of theological reasons, but its application emphasizes the need for regular church attendance. Grant Osborne rightly claimed that cultural and historical knowledge would transform a sermon from a two-dimensional study to a three-dimensional cinematic event.[ii] Historically, the setting in this passage is important because it describes a series of problematic events that early Christians struggled with in ancient Rome that created problems in the church. For example, the Roman historian, Suetonius, described an edict that forced Christian believers from their homes in A.D. 49. The edict became known as the *Edict of Claudius* and came about over a disturbance by the Jews over one known as "Chrestus."[iii] The term "Chrestus" is only one letter off from the Latin "Christus," meaning Christ, to whom many scholars believe Suetonius was referring.

Claudius died in A.D. 54, and this led to the rise of one of the most hated Caesars in history, the emperor Nero. Nero's persecutions were notorious and ranged from viciously attacking people on the streets at night,[iv] to murdering his aunt,[v] and to blaming the Christians for setting fire to the city.[vi] As a result, some of the Christians began attending services at the Jewish synagogues, instead of attending church, in an effort to escape persecution. All of these events, from the *Edict of Claudius* to Nero's persecutions, culminated in a setting where Christian church attendance in Rome had begun to wane, and this had a horrific impact on their ability to grow and mature in their faith. This leads to the main point of this passage. The author of Hebrews encourages believers to press on toward maturity, or to grow spiritually, so they will not be sluggish in their faith but be Christians who inherit the promises of God through faith and patience.

Before we exegete the passage, we must first identify some literary devices that set the boundaries for this passage and also clarify the context. Ancient biblical authors sometimes used rare words to mark the beginning and ending points of a passage; words that frame passages are referred to as an "*inclusio*" and are used to mark the boundaries of a passage.[vii] The Greek word *nothroi* is used only twice in the entire New Testament, but is found in Hebrews 5:11 and 6:12. Therefore, it is not a coincidence that the author of Hebrews surrounds a story emphasizing a progression from laziness to spiritual growth by using a word that is typically translated as sluggish or dull.[viii]

In addition to grasping the boundaries of the passage, the pastor/teacher must learn to recognize particular literary devices used in Scripture. Osborne commented, "The best illustrations come not from cute stories or clever repartee but from the text itself."[ix] Verses 6:7-8 are significant for interpretation, since the author uses metaphor to describe the problem that all spiritually immature believers struggle with. The metaphorical reference of a ground that drinks the rain, which in turn produces vegetation, is another way of talking about bearing fruit, and this stands in contrast to a ground that produces only thorns and thistles. The author of Hebrews is contrasting mature, fruit-bearing believers with immature believers who do not bear fruit.

The failure to grow from a spiritual perspective has been taken up before by the author of Hebrews in 3:7-12, where he used the wilderness generation from the Old Testament as an example of people who lacked faithful obedience and failed to grow spiritually. They became disobedient due to their lack of faith, as a result of their spiritual immaturity. The progression grew worse as their apostasy spread to the entire community.[x] In 3:12, the author then warns the Christians of Rome to guard themselves and commands them not to fall away from a living God.

There are two verbs that are significant in this verse. First is the Greek verb translated by the NASB as "take care," and this verb is typically translated as "see" (*blepo*). The verb is used in an imperative form; the author is commanding them to look at their relationships with God and evaluate them. Growing, maturing relationships with our Lord come about from on-going efforts to seek our Lord's guidance and wisdom and requires far more than simply making a profession of faith.

The second verb (*apostanai*) in verse twelve is translated by the NASB as "falling away," and our English word apostasy comes from this verb. Some New Testament scholars claim the author of Hebrews was not discussing the possibility of an apostasy, but was, rather, urging these believers to examine the condition of their faith and the repercussions of not moving toward maturity.[xi] This notion actually works against what the Scripture itself says, since the word apostasy is used in the text. Ben Witherington described a growing faith by using the analogy of riding a bicycle.[xii] Just as a cyclist is able to take his hands off of the handlebars as long as he/she is moving forward, believers are able to grow in their faith as long as we are moving forward. The problem comes when the cyclist tries to stop, and then falls over. Likewise, when the Christians in Rome stopped growing or moving forward in their faith, they fell away into apostasy or unbelief. From this perspective, the wilderness generation becomes the epitome of a people that failed to grow and believe, and they paid a hefty price for their disobedience. Just as the wilderness generation forfeited their inheritance of entering into the Promised Land because of their unbelief, the Christians in Rome during this time stand to forfeit an even greater inheritance; namely salvation, because of their apostasy and unbelief.

As a result of this setting, the author of Hebrews makes three sub-points. First, he identifies a problem in their faith. This sub-point is supported in 5:11, where he says they have become dull of hearing or slow to learn.[xiii] By this time, they ought to be teachers. Spiritual immaturity is described metaphorically in 5:11-14 as a result of having ears that do not hear. No Christian ever aspires to become dull of hearing; they become this way by failing to persevere in their faith. Use of the perfect tense for the word "become" supports this notion, since a perfect tense verb indicates a past action with consequences that are felt in the speaker's present time.[xiv] The past action was the decision these believers had made to stop attending church services, and the effects of sporadic church attendance had a horrific impact on spiritual growth. Pastors see the results of this spiritual immaturity with people who have failed to grow and regularly create division in the church.

The second sub-point the author of Hebrews makes is that he recommends a solution to the problem, and this sub-point is supported by 6:1 where he encourages believers to press on toward maturity or toward perfection. The Greek verb translated as "press on" is from the lexical form of the word *phero* and literally means to "carry" as in carry on. Our English word "ferry" or a boat that carries vehicles across a body of water comes from this word. Also, the verb is used in a present tense that denotes a continuous type of action.[xv] The author of Hebrews is talking about the on-going effort of pressing on or carrying on toward maturity.

In addition to grammar that describes an on-going effort to grow from a spiritual perspective, the author of Hebrews also describes a process of leaving behind particular issues that are elementary in nature. These are issues dealing with baptisms, the laying on of hands, resurrection from the dead, and judgment. While they are an integral part of the Christian faith, they are also elementary in the sense that they are for those who have not yet grown to full maturity.

Finally, the author of Hebrews encourages believers to move on to a path of spiritual growth, and this is supported by 6:11-12. Encouraging believers to a path of spiritual growth was a common form of rhetoric in the ancient world. The author's desire was that they not remain sluggish or dull of hearing but that they make a conscious effort to allow God into their lives to build their faith.

GROUNDED: *Anchoring the Evangelical Sermon in Theological Doctrine*

My first Greek professor in seminary once told the story about his childhood and how he had grown up in a rural area in Georgia. He joined the Navy in WWII, and before they shipped out, their unit docked in one of the harbors in New York for a few days of rest and recreation. As a boy who was raised in rural Georgia, he was anxious to see and tour some of the skyscrapers in the city. While touring the Empire State Building, he met one of the engineers who assisted in the design and construction of the building, and he asked him a question, "How does a building this tall continue to stand and keep from falling?" The engineer responded that much of New York City is solid rock, and when the engineers pour a foundation, they anchor it to the ground by drilling holes at each corner and placing thirty-foot spikes to anchor the foundation. "Since the ground is solid rock," the engineer said, "you could erect a building a high as you wanted, and it would not fall."

Down the street from the Empire State Building, construction for a new sky scraper had begun, and the foundation had already been poured, but when WWII came, supplies were rationed, and the construction was postponed. Instead, a tiny storage shed was erected in the middle of this massive foundation.

My professor then made this analogy: these two buildings are quite similar to the Christian faith. Just as these skyscrapers included massive foundations, Christians have the same massive foundation to build upon. While the foundations of these buildings were anchored to solid rock, the Christian faith is also anchored to belief in the solid rock of Jesus Christ. Upon these foundations, some of us choose to build skyscrapers, and some of us choose to build tiny storage sheds. He then asked me this somber question: What will you choose to build upon your foundation? Will you be someone who towers in your faith like the skyscrapers, or will you be someone who is content to erect a tiny storage shed? This question continues to resonate in my heart even today and regularly pushes me from a path of spiritual laziness.

So much of the Christian faith in North America is embodied in this analogy. All too often, Christians take the easy route in life that does not require much from us. We erect our tiny storage sheds of faith by dabbling in Christianity but never truly invest ourselves in faith and Christian service. Then we wonder why our faith does not sustain us during times of trial. In doing so, we become the same stunted believers the author of Hebrews warns against.

David W. Brown

Growing Up or Growing Old:
The Lifelong Process of Spiritual Maturity
Hebrews 5:11-6:12

INTRODUCTION:

Setting:
On-going persecutions from the Roman emperors had a horrific impact on spiritual growth for Christians. As a result, church attendance had begun to wane.

<u>Examples</u>:
* The Edict of Claudius in A.D. 49
* Nero's Persecution in A.D. 54-68

Main Point:
The author of Hebrews encourages believers to press on toward maturity so they will not be sluggish or dull of hearing.

Structure:
There is a chapter division in the middle of this passage. The Greek word *nothroi* forms an *inclusio* and frames the passage.

Warning:
The author of Hebrews has already warned believers in 3:7-12 about committing an apostasy and forfeiting their inheritance:
* The Wilderness Generation is used as a poor example of people who fell into apostasy and unbelief.
* Faith is much like riding a bicycle: As long as we are moving forward (growing), we are ok, but when we try to stop, we lose our balance and fall.

BODY:

Sub-Points:

  I. The author identifies a problem with their faith (5:11).

   A) Believers have become dull of hearing or sluggish in their faith.

   i. They ought to be teachers by now, but they need someone to teach them the elementary principles of the faith.

GROUNDED: *Anchoring the Evangelical Sermon in Theological Doctrine*

  ii. Spiritual immaturity is described metaphorically as having ears that do not hear.
 B) The Greek word for "become" is a perfect tense that denotes a past action with lasting consequences.
  i. The past action in the context of the passage was the decision to stop going to church, where they would learn and grow in their faith.
  ii. Their failure to endure persecution and continue to attend church had a horrific impact on their spiritual growth.

II. **The author recommends a solution (6:1).**
 A) The solution to the problem is to press on toward maturity.
  i. The Greek verb *phero* is translated as press on or carry on. Our English word ferry comes from this word.
  ii. The verb is used in a present tense form that denotes a continuous action–the author is talking about a continuous effort to grow or carry on spiritually.
 B) He also recommends leaving behind elementary teachings that are for beginners in the faith.
  i. Aiding the process of spiritual growth:
   1. Go to church.
   2. Study your Bible daily.
   3. Plug into Christian service in your church.

III. **The author encourages believers to follow a path of spiritual growth (6:11-12).**
 A) Tell the story of Dr. A. growing up in GA:
  * He joined the Navy during WWII.
  * They stopped in New York harbor before shipping out.
  * While touring the Empire State Building, he asked an engineer a question.
  * How does a building this tall keep from falling over?
  * New York is mostly solid rock.
  * Workers pour foundations and drill 30 ft. spike into the ground to anchor it.
  * Down the street, another sky scraper was being built.
  * WWII caused supplies to be rationed.
  * Foundation had already been poured–workers erected a tiny storage shed in the middle of the foundation.

* Both of these foundations are similar to the Christian faith.
* Believers also have a solid foundation anchor to the solid rock of Jesus Christ.
* Upon these foundations some of us choose to build skyscrapers and some of us choose to build tiny storage sheds.
* What path will you choose?
  - Will we build skyscrapers or storage sheds?

SUMMATION:

This is a passage that teaches believers they must grow to full maturity to guard against falling away from the faith. The author does this by: identifying a problem, making a recommendation, and encouraging them to follow the path of Christian maturity.

Final Thoughts:

In order to understand this passage and grasp the author's message, the reader must first identify the boundaries of where this passage begins and ends. This is made all the more difficult, since a chapter division falls in the middle of this passage and interrupts the emphasis the author is making. Therefore, proper interpretation must come by identifying the literary markers that set the boundaries for this passage. When I preach this passage, I make a point to note the problems the chapter division created with respect to proper interpretation.

This is a passage that emphasizes the need for regular church attendance, as well as believers' need to grow to full maturity. Evangelicals must be pushed from a spiritual perspective to deeper understandings of the Bible, and this will never happen with sporadic church attendance and priorities that place God and service well down the list of things-to-do in life. God's desire is for believers to humbly commit themselves in service to our Lord Jesus by committing themselves to the hard work of theological study.

---

[i]Metzger, *Manuscripts*, 42.

[ii]Osborne, *Spiral*, 158

[iii]Suetonius, *The Twelve Caesars*, (London: Penguin Books Publishing, 2003), 201.

[iv]Ibid., 227.

[v]Ibid., 233.

[vi]Ibid., 236.

[vii]G. H. Guthrie, "*The Structure of Hebrews: A Text-Linguistic Analysis*" (Grand Rapids: Baker Books Publishing, 1994).

[viii]William L. Lane, "*Word Biblical Commentary Hebrews 1-8 vol. 47a*" (Grand Rapids: Thomas Nelson Publishing, 1991), 136.

[ix]Osborne, *Spiral*, 130.

[x]Gary M. Burge, Lynn H. Cohick, Gene L. Green, "*The New Testament in Antiquity: A Survey of the New Testament within its Cultural Contexts*" (Grand Rapids: Zondervan Publishing, 2009), 389-90.

[xi]Andreas J. Köstenberger, L. Scott Kellum, Charles L. Quarels, "*The Cradle, the Cross, and the Crown: An introduction to the New Testament*" (Nashville: B & H Academic Publishing, 2009), 695.

[xii]Ben Witherington, *The Problem with Evangelical Theology: Testing the Exegetical Foundations of Calvinism, Dispensationalism, and Wesleyanism* (Waco: Baylor University Press, 2005), 145.

[xiii]Donald A. Hagner, *Encountering the Book of Hebrews* (Grand Rapids: Baker Academic Publishing, 2002), 85.

[xiv]William D. Mounce, *Basics of Biblical Greek Grammar* 3rd ed. (Grand Rapids: Zondervan Publishing, 2009), 222.

[xv]Mounce, *Basics*, 257.

David W. Brown

Chapter 2

Colossians 1:3 - 14
Commentary and Interpretation

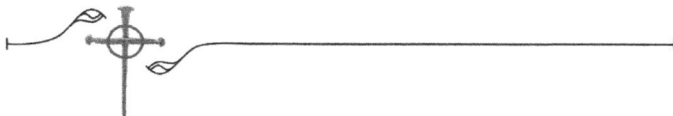

Great sermons come about by recognizing literary devices that were built into the text of the Bible that can transform your sermon from a Bible study into a homiletical masterpiece. Unfortunately, many of these literary devices are difficult to recognize once translated into English. Books that point out these literary features are an essential part of sermon preparation.[i]

This passage is a combination of two paragraphs, and the temptation for pastors is to rush to the commentaries too soon to read the explanations for the verses, which causes them to miss the literary features in the text. These paragraphs should be interpreted together, and there are several literary features that support this rationale. First, as Gordon Fee pointed out, verses three through fourteen are a single sentence in the Greek New Testament.[ii] Second, the passage begins in verse three and ends in verse fourteen with the word for thanksgiving,[iii] framing the passage with the concept of thanksgiving.[iv] In addition, there are two important literary movements employed in this passage that anchor the theological message of the book. Paul places both of these movements in verses twelve and thirteen:[v]

    1) The movement from you[vi] (*humas*) to us (*hemas*)
    2) The movement from Father to Son

As a result of these literary and grammatical devices, these two paragraphs function together in an organized effort to emphasize the work the Father has done through the Son. At the same time, the Colossian believers are called to give thanks to the Father for that work.

The purpose of the book is a Christ-centered correction to Colossian errorists who had deviated from an orthodox path by blending together various Jewish and pagan beliefs into their understanding of Christianity.[vii] For this reason, Paul writes the book of Colossians for the express purpose of grounding believers in a solid theological understanding of the Christian faith. At the heart of the message are some who have erred and desire to regulate the Christian life by a set of external codes.[viii] Speculations abound as to the identity of what group Paul was describing, but the significance of these regulations "do not handle," "do not taste," and "do not touch" is that they were impacting the Colossians' understanding of the Christian faith in a ritualistic and negative way (2:21).

This leads to the main point of the passage: Paul seeks, through intercessory prayer, to steer the faith of the Colossian believers by turning their attention to heavenly things, namely the atoning work of Jesus, who transferred them from the dominion of darkness into the light of Christ and his heavenly kingdom. This monumental transfer calls for joyous thanksgiving to their heavenly Father for the work he has accomplished through his son Jesus.

The first sub-point of this passage is that Paul gives thanks to God by praying for the spiritual growth of other believers, and this sub-point is supported by verses three through six. This sub-point is difficult to locate and put together, since Paul has spread the point across three verses interlaced with rhetorical phrases derived from the Hellenistic period.[ix] Nonetheless, the point can be seen:

* Giving thanks to the Father while praying for you always (1:3)
* Through the hope being laid up for you which is the gospel (1:5)
* Coming to you and the whole world, it is bearing fruit and growing (1:6)

Paul is giving thanks to God through prayer that the gospel message laid up for the Colossians bears fruit and continues to grow. The intensity of Paul's prayer for their spiritual growth is illustrated by the use of two present tense participles for the words "growing" (*karpophoroumenon*) and "bearing fruit" (*auxonomenon*). Present tense participles are built on the present tense stem of the verb and indicate a continuous action,[x] so Paul is talking about on-going spiritual growth that bears fruit regularly.

Spiritual growth is essential for believers to come to full maturity. Christians can hold great theological views about God, but if we are not applying them to our lives for spiritual growth, then we are not giving proper thanks to God. A quote from Will Rodgers captures the idea; "Even if you are on the right track, you will get run over if you just sit there."[xi] The point Paul is making is that giving thanks to God is not just a phrase we think about when we close our prayers. By contrast, one of the greatest ways believers can give thanks to God is by living a life marked by the obedience of spiritual maturity.

The second sub-point is Paul prays that the Colossians are filled with wisdom and spiritual insight that lead to Godly conduct, and this sub-point is supported by verses nine and ten. The intensity of Paul's prayers are emphasized by the use of two present middle participles, both for praying (*proseuchomenoi*) and asking (*aitoumenoi*) that denote on-going prayer and on-going asking.[xii] Also, the word for filled (*plerothete*) is an aorist passive, which means the subject receives the action of the verb.[xiii] The context of the passage implies that God is the one doing the filling. Thus, Paul is praying to God and asking him to fill the Colossian believers with knowledge of his will.

This sub-point supports the fact that Christian believers are not simply to live as repositories of knowledge. Grant Osborne rightly states, "We can spend hours immersed in academic pursuit of exegetical knowledge but yet fail to truly know, because knowledge rather than Christ is on the throne of our lives."[xiv] The Godly wisdom that Paul is praying for is wisdom that changes the way the Colossian believers are living for God. In other words, Paul is praying and asking God to fill these believers with knowledge of his will for the expressed purpose of deriving wisdom from it that changes the way they live as Christians.

The third sub-point is that Paul gives thanks to God for including the Gentile believers into his kingdom, and this is supported by verses twelve through fourteen. One of the larger problems inherent in religious life is the tendency to see ourselves superior to those outside of the faith, and this attitude of superiority causes believers to hesitate in reaching out to those who are different from us. Jim Cymbala emphasized this very point in a moving story in his book *Fresh Wind, Fresh Fire*. He wrote:

> I shall never forget Easter Sunday 1992—the day Roberta Langella gave her dramatic testimony. A homeless man was standing in the back of the church listening intently.
>
> At the end of the evening meeting, I sat down on the edge of the platform, exhausted, as others continued to pray with those who responded to Christ. The organist was playing quietly. I wanted to relax. I was just starting to unwind when I looked up to see this man with shabby clothing and matted hair standing in the center isle about four rows back waiting for permission to approach me.
>
> I nodded and gave him a weak little wave of my hand. Look at how this Easter Sunday is going to end, I thought to myself. He is going to hit me for money. This happens often in this church. I'm so tired...
>
> When he came close, I saw that two front teeth were missing. But more striking was his odor-the mixture of alcohol, sweat, urine, and garbage took my breath away. I have been around many street people, but this was the strongest stench I have ever encountered. I instinctively had to turn my head to inhale, then look back in his direction while breathing out.
>
> I asked his name.
>
> "David," he said softly.
>
> "How long have you been homeless, David?"
>
> "Six years."
>
> "Where did you sleep last night?"
>
> "In an abandoned truck."
>
> I had heard enough and wanted to get this over quickly. I reached for the money clip in my back pocket.
>
> At that moment, David put his finger in front of my face and said, "No, you don't understand—I don't want your money. I'm going to die out there. I want the Jesus that red haired girl talked about."
>
> I hesitated, then closed my eyes. God forgive me, I begged. I felt soiled and cheap. Me, a minister of the gospel...I had simply wanted to get rid of him, when he was crying out for the help

of Christ I had just preached about. I swallowed hard as God's love flooded my soul.

David sensed the change in me. He moved toward me and fell on my chest, burying his grimy head against my white shirt and tie. Holding him close, I talked to him about Jesus' love. These weren't just words; I felt them. I felt love for this pitiful young man. And that smell...I don't know how to explain it. It had almost made me sick, but now it became the most beautiful fragrance to me. I reveled in what had been repulsive just a moment ago.

The Lord seemed to say to me in that instant. Jim, if you and your wife have any value to me, if you have any purpose in my work—it has to do with this odor. This is the smell of the world I died for.[xv]

Christianity is not about the work we do, but it is about plugging into the work God has already done (i.e. plugging into God's redemptive plan), and one of the greatest ways of giving thanks to God for the work he has done is by living a life inviting people into the Christian fold. In doing so, we extend the same grace to them that God has extended to us.

David W. Brown

Thanksgiving and Christian Living:
Giving Thanks to the Father for the Work He has Accomplished through His Son
Colossians 1:3-14

INTRODUCTION:
Main Point:
Paul seeks, by intercessory prayer, to steer the faith of the Colossian believers to focus on heavenly things, namely the atoning work of Jesus, who transferred them from darkness into the light of His eternal kingdom.

Structure:
The passage is composed of two paragraphs that should be interpreted together:
* Verses three through fourteen are all a single sentence in the Greek.
* The passage is framed by the word "thanksgiving."
* Two literary movements anchor the passage: (1:12-13)
    * From you (*humas*) to us (*hemas*)
    * From Father to Son

Structural Application:
The result of these literary and grammatical devices is a passage where both paragraphs function together in an effort to emphasize the Father's work through the Son. The Colossian believers are called to give thanks to the Father for his work.

Purpose:
The author of Colossians sends a Christ-centered correction to the Colossian errorists who have deviated from an orthodox path by blending together various Jewish and pagan beliefs in their understanding of Christianity.

BODY:
Sub-Points:
- I. Paul gives thanks to God by praying for spiritual growth of the Colossian believers (1:3-6).
    - A) Paul gives thanks to God that the gospel message laid up for the Colossians bears fruit and continues to grow.
        - i. The intensity of Paul's prayer is reflected in the use of two present tense participles, both for "bearing fruit" (*karpophoroumenon*) and "growing" (*auxonomenon*).
        - ii. Present tense participles denote continuous action, so we are talking about on-going spiritual growth that leads to regular, fruit-bearing efforts.
    - B) Regular spiritual growth requires effort on the part of the believer.
        - i. Will Rodgers once said, "Even if you are on the right track, you will get run over if you just sit there."
- II. Paul prays that the Colossians are filled with wisdom and spiritual insight that leads to godly conduct (1:9-10).
    - A) The intensity of Paul's prayers is denoted by two present tense participles (praying and asking):
        - i. Present tense participles denote a continuous type of action, so Paul is talking about regularly lifting up the Colossians in his prayers and asking God to fill them with His wisdom and all spiritual insight.
        - ii. Christians are not to live as simply repositories of knowledge but are called to use knowledge about God to edify themselves and others.
    - B) The Greek word for filled is a passive voice verb and that teaches that believers are the recipients of that action.
        - i. The context indicates that God is the one doing the filling.
    - C) The point is that a solid understanding of God leads to a solid living for God.
        - i. Paul is praying for the Colossians to be filled by God with wisdom and spiritual insight that will lead to Godly conduct in how they live.
- III. Paul gives thanks to God for including the Gentile believers into his kingdom (1:12-14).

      A) One of the problems in religious life is the tendency to see ourselves superior to those outside of the faith.
         i. This attitude of superiority often keeps us from reaching out to people who are different from us.
      B) Tell the story by Jim Cymbala (see commentary).
      C) Christianity is not about the work we do but is about plugging in to the work God has already done (i.e. plugging in to God's redemptive plan).
         i. The greatest way of giving thanks to God for the work he has done is by living a life inviting people into the Christian fold.
         ii. In doing so, we extend the same grace to them that God has extended to us.

SUMMATION:

This is a passage about giving thanks to God for the work he has accomplished through his son Jesus Christ. The passage reflects Paul's fervent intercessory prayer on behalf of the Colossians that God fill them with his wisdom and spiritual insight. In doing so, this wisdom will transform their lives into lives of humility by extending to others the same grace God has extended to us.

Final Thoughts:

The importance of understanding how these two paragraphs function cannot be overestimated. Picking up on these literary and grammatical features is crucial for proper interpretation of this passage. Far too often, believers attempt to insert their opinions and works into the Christian faith (as the Colossians were doing), and in doing so, they turn Christianity into a faith that is all about themselves. This passage teaches believers that Christianity centers more on the work of what the Father has done through his Son than the work believers accomplish.

---

[i] J. Scott Duvall, J. Daniel Hays, *Grasping God's Word: A Hands-On Approach to Reading, Interpreting, and Applying the Bible* 2nd ed. (Grand Rapids: Zondervan Publishing, 2005). See also Terry G. Carter, J. Scott Duvall, J. Daniel Hays, *Preaching God's Word: A Hands-On Approach to Preparing, Developing, and Delivering the Sermon* (Grand Rapids: Zondervan Publishing, 2005).

[ii] Gordon D. Fee, *Pauline Christology: An Exegetical-Theological Study* (Peabody: Hendrickson Publishers, 2007), 294.

[iii] Ibid.

[iv] Peter T. O'Brien, *Introductory Thanksgiving in the Letters of Paul* (Eugene: Wipf and Stock Publishing, 1977), 62-104.

[v] Fee, *Pauline Christology*, 294.

[vi] Chrys C. Caragounis, *The Development of Greek and the New Testament: Morphology, Syntax, Phonology, and Textual Transmission* (Grand Rapids: Baker Academic Publishing, 2006), 517-46. The confusion between the pronouns you (*humas*) and us (*hemas*) is explained in detail by the interchange of various Greek vowels that produced similar sounds. These are referred to as orthographic or hearing differences.

[vii] Köstenberger, Kellum, Quarels, *The Cradle*, 609-10.

[viii] Gordon D. Fee, Douglas Stuart, *How to Read the Bible Book by Book: A Guided Tour* (Grand Rapids: Zondervan Publishing, 2002), 360.

[ix] Peter T. O'Brien, *Word Biblical Commentary: Colossians, Philemon* (Grand Rapids: Thomas Nelson Publishers, 1982), 7-8.

[x] Mounce, *Basics*, 245.

[xi] Dole, *Hearts*, 19.

[xii] Mounce, *Basics*, 245.

[xiii] Ibid. 149.

[xiv] Osborne, *Spiral*, 137.

[xv] Jim Cymbala, *Fresh Wind, Fresh Fire* (Grand Rapids: Zondervan, 1997), 141-43.

David W. Brown

Chapter 3

Philippians 2:1 - 11
Commentary and Interpretation

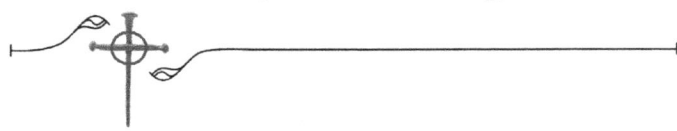

Great sermons teach believers that how we think about God is reflected in how we live our lives for him. In my years of serving as a pastor, I have heard this passage preached many times and have yet to hear the passage preached in its proper context. In most cases, the pastor began his/her preaching with verse five and typically emphasized the need to live a life as modeled in this passage by Jesus. This is good and proper exegesis; unfortunately, the beginning of the passage has been regularly left off, but it forms a crucial part of interpretation.

Have you ever been asked to perform a task you were not sure how to do? How would you have felt if, the moment after making a profession of faith, one of the pastors in your church came to you and asked you to teach an in-depth Bible study on the book of Revelation? Most would be apprehensive, and rightfully so, because new Christians do not have a strong understanding of the Bible and would therefore fail miserably at the task, since they had not been trained for it. This is why the first four verses of this passage are so important, because Paul uses them to tell the believers in Caesarea Philippi that if we are going to live like Christ, we must first learn how to think like him.

Although Caesarea Philippi was a Roman province during Jesus' ministry, the population of the city was most likely a mixture of both Jewish and a variety of Gentile backgrounds.[i] However, pagan belief was rampant in Caesarea Philippi where an underground stream had surfaced and still exists today.[ii] Tradition held this underground stream was one of the gateways to the underworld and the river of Styx.[iii] The pagan traditions held in Caesarea Philippi serve only to heighten the emphasis Paul is making: proper thinking about God leads to a proper living for God.

The organization of the passage is significant, since it is made up of two paragraphs: [iv]

* Philippians 2:1-4 teaches believers how to think like Christ
* Philippians 2:5-11 teaches believers how to live like Christ

Paul places these two paragraphs back-to-back in an organized effort to teach the Philippian believers that Godly thinking leads to Godly living. This can be a double-edged sword, since a sloppy understanding of God leads to sloppy living for him; by contrast, solid understanding of God leads to a solid living for God. Therefore, Paul's mission is to encourage the believers in Philippi to come to a proper understanding of God that will, in turn, lead them to a proper living for him.

Examples of Godly thinking that lead to Godly living are found throughout the first two chapters of the book of Philippians, and Paul goes to great lengths to list these examples in the larger context of this passage. Throughout these chapters, Paul cites repeated examples of those who modeled this behavior throughout both their lives and ministries.

1. The Example of Paul (1:12-30)
2. The Example of Christ (2:1-11)
3. The Example of Timothy (2:19-24)
4. The Example of Epaphroditus (2:25-30)[v]

In each of these passages, Paul lists examples of those whose lives reflected a proper understanding of God that permeated the way they lived. Each example illustrates those who put the Father's will first in their lives, with Christ being the highlight and focal point of the examples.

One of the literary features the pastor/teacher must note in this passage is how often the Greek verb *phroneo* is used. This verb is translated in a variety of ways, but context in this passage indicates the word means to "think."[vi] This is crucial for interpretation, since word repetition has a cumulative type of effect that places an emphasis on understanding the larger context. The word *phroneo* is repeated four times from verses two through five,[vii] and this shows that Paul is clearly placing an emphasis on this word.

GROUNDED: *Anchoring the Evangelical Sermon in Theological Doctrine*

In addition, the verb is used in verse five to tie the two paragraphs together and also to command believers to make themselves think like Christ, since Paul uses the verb in an imperative form.[viii] This leads us to Paul's main point of the passage, and that is if believers are going to live like Christ, we must first learn how to think like him. Christians have often used the acrostic WWJD that asks the question "What Would Jesus Do?" However, if we were to emphasize Paul's meaning in this passage, we most likely would change the acrostic to WWJT or "What Would Jesus Think?"

The first sub-point is that Godly thinking means placing others' needs before our own, and this is supported by verse one. Notice how Paul piles up the nouns in this verse in an effort to emphasize that believers are to place the needs of others ahead of their own. When the biblical writers list a series of nouns one after another, the compounding effect is to place an emphasis.[ix] This compounding emphasis can be seen below:

* Encouragement in Christ
* Consolation of love (also known as empathy)
* Fellowship of the spirit
* Affection
* Compassion

In the context of this passage, Paul lists five attributes in rapid-fire succession that will not only shape the character of the believer but will enable them to live in a sacrificial manner, just as Jesus did.

The second sub-point that Paul makes is that Godly thinking leads to Godly living, and this is supported by verse five, where Paul commands the Philippians to think like Christ. The repetition of the word "think" has already been noted, but Paul makes this point crystal clear in verse five by commanding the Philippians to think like Christ. If preachers use PowerPoint presentations in their sermons, it should emphasize Paul's repetition:

* Make my joy complete by **thinking** the same thing (2:2a)
* Be joined together in soul by **thinking** the same thing (2:2b)
* With humility in the way we **think** (2:3)
* Make your own **thinking** to be like that of Christ Jesus (2:5)[x]

Verses that use repetition place an emphasis in the text and are also designed to challenge the Philippian believers to push themselves to think in a sacrificial manner, just as Christ did. Christians need to be challenged from a theological standpoint. All too often, believers look for the easy route in life. We constantly seek the downhill path that does not require anything from us. However, Christian believers need to be challenged to think about Christ in ways that push us and shape the character of who we are as believers.

When believers commit themselves to think like Christ, the Devil will put opposition in our paths to prevent us from growing to spiritual maturity. There is a great quote by Robert F. Kennedy that pertains to challenges and opposition: "If there is nobody in your way, it's because you're not going anywhere."[xi] The same idea applies to believers today. Great spiritual growth is always met with opposition. Christ commands believers to make ourselves think like Christ in a way that leads us to live for him.

The third sub-point that Paul makes is that Godly thinking begins by exalting Jesus as the Lord of our lives, and this is supported by verses nine through eleven. The Greek's use of rhetoric to persuade their audience of the truth of their message was common in the ancient world.[xii] Paul used the same rhetoric to persuade his readers to confess Jesus to be Lord of their lives:

* God highly exalted him (2:9a)
* His name is above every name (2:9b)
* Every knee will bow (2:10)
* Every tongue confess (2:11)

The concept here is that Christians need to be bold in their speech that Christ is our Lord. Being bold does not mean that we must be abrupt or obnoxious. In fact, I am convinced that we can boldly proclaim Jesus to be our Lord even in a gentle voice.

As a pastor, I visit homebound members on a regular basis. Many of these folks are members who were once very active in church, but now, due to health issues, have limited mobility and can rarely attend services. While visiting one of our members, my friend Ted recounted the story from years earlier of how he had once met Corrie ten Boom. He was in the

Chicago airport and had a layover of a few of hours before his flight. While waiting, Ted had occupied his time by reading her book *"The Hiding Place,"* and the edition he had been reading had her picture on the back cover. During this time, he had noticed a woman sitting across from him who looked remarkably like Corrie ten Boom. Back and forth he went, looking at the picture on the cover of the book and then again at the woman. After some time, his curiosity got the better of him and Ted walked over and asked the woman "Are you Corrie ten Boom?"

With a warm smile, the woman looked up and replied, "I am, do you happen to know my Lord?" I often think about Corrie's humble response. At that moment, she had the opportunity to bask in her fame, a fame that many would have claimed she had rightly earned, but without hesitation, she laid it, like a rose, at the foot of our Lord. Corrie ten Boom had mastered the art of boldly confessing Jesus to be her Lord in a very gentle way.

David W. Brown

WWJT:
Godly Thinking that Leads to Godly Living
Philippians 2:1-11

INTRODUCTION:
Structure:
    The passage is organized into two distinct paragraphs that teach that Godly thinking leads to Godly living:
        * Philippians 1-4 teaches believers how to think like Christ.
        * Philippians 5-11 teaches believers how to live like Christ.

Organization:
    The larger context of the passage lists four examples of those whose lives reflected a proper understanding of God that permeated the way they lived:
      1. The Example of Paul (1:12-30)
      2. The Example of Christ (2:1-11)
      3. The Example of Timothy (2:19-24)
      4. The Example of Epaphroditus (2:25-30)

Main Point:
    If believers are going to live like Christ, we must first learn how to think like him.

Acrostic:
    Christians often use the acrostic WWJD that asks the question "What Would Jesus Do?" but if we are going to emphasize Paul's application to the passage, we should modify the acrostic to WWJT "What Would Jesus Think?"

BODY:
Sub-Points:

    I. Godly thinking means placing others' needs before our own (2:1-4).
      A. Paul piles the nouns in order to emphasize how believers can live like Christ by placing others' needs ahead of our own.

         i. These attributes shape the character of the believer into one who lives like Christ.
         ii. Encouragement, consolation of love (also known as empathy), fellowship, affection, and compassion are all attributes that, when applied to our lives, reflect those who live like Christ.
II. **Godly thinking leads to godly living (2:5).**
   A. The Greek word (*phroneo*) to think is repeated four times in five verses.
      i. The emphasis of the repetition should be noted:
         * Make my joy complete by thinking the same thing (2:2a)
         * Be joined together in soul by thinking the same thing (2:2b)
         * With humility in the way we think (2:3)
         * Make your own thinking be like that of Christ Jesus (2:5)
   B. When believers begin to think and live like Christ, the Devil will place others before us who will oppose us at every turn.
      i. Robert F. Kennedy once said: "If there is nobody in your way, it's because you are not going anywhere."
III. **Godly thinking begins by exalting Jesus to be Lord of our lives (2:9-11).**
   A. The Greeks used rhetoric to persuade their audience of the truth of their message.
      i. Believers can proclaim Jesus to be their Lord in gentle ways.
      ii. Tell the story of Corrie ten Boom:
         * As a pastor, I visit the homebound on a regular basis.
         * One of our members told me the story of meeting Corrie ten Boom.
         * He had a layover in the Chicago airport.
         * He had bought her book "The Hiding Place" to pass the time.
         * The copy Ted was reading had her picture on the back cover.
         * During his layover he noticed a woman on in the airport who looked remarkably like Corrie ten Boom.
         * After a while, Ted's curiosity got the better of him.
         * He walked over and asked the lady if she was Corrie ten Boom?

* She responded, "I am, do you happen to know my Lord?"
* Corrie was boldly proclaiming Christ to be her Lord in a very gentle way.

SUMMATION:

This passage teaches believers that if we are going to live like Christ, we must first learn how to think like him. This is a passage that teaches:

I. Godly thinking means putting others' needs ahead of our own.
II. Godly thinking leads to Godly living.
III. Godly thinking exalts Jesus as Lord.

Final Thoughts:

Grammatical emphasis is important for a congregation to learn. Christian views are held because the Scripture itself supports that view. The use of history, grammar, and theology in a sermon grounds the believer in a proper understanding of what the author is emphasizing in the passage. Sermons that are grounded in solid exegesis guard against the idea that every view is a valid one. If our theological understandings of a given passage are not supported by the historical and grammatical emphasis placed on the text, then we must rework our understanding of the passage in accordance to what the Bible teaches.

If the congregation is going to grasp the meaning of this passage, the repetition Paul is placing on "thinking like Christ" must be noted. How we think about God reflects in how we live our lives for him. If we have a sloppy understanding of God, this will lead to a sloppy living for God. By contrast, a proper understanding of God leads to a proper living for God.

---

[i] Peter T. O'Brien, *The New International Greek Testament Commentary: The Epistle to the Philippians* (Grand Rapids: William B. Eerdmans Publishing, 1991), 4.

[ii] Ben Witherington, *What Have They Done With Jesus: Beyond strange theories and bad history – Why we can trust the Bible* (New York: Harper SanFrancisco Publishing, 2006), 63.

[iii] Ibid.

[iv] Both the *Nestle-Aland Novum Testamentum Graece* 27th edition and the *United Bible Society's* 4th edition place paragraph markers at verses 1 and 5.

[v] Köstenberger, Kellum, Quarels, *The Cradle*, 569-70.

[vi] Lynn H. Cohick, "The Complete Work of Christ" in *Devotions on the Greek New Testament: 52 Reflections to Inspire & Instruct.* ed. J. Scott Duvall & Verlyn D. Verbrugge. Grand Rapids: Zondervan Publishing. 2012, p. 91-94.

[vii] Warren C. Trenchard, *Complete Vocabulary Guide to the Greek New Testament* Revised Edition (Grand Rapids: Zondervan Publishing, 1998), 119. The word translated in verse three by the NIV as "humility" or the NASB as "humility of mind" is the compound word *tapenophrosune*. This Greek verb is a combination of *tapeinos* and *phren* with *phren* belonging to the same cognate group as *phroneo*. The context denotes the idea of humility in our thoughts or humility in the way we think.

[viii] Mounce, *Basics*, 309-17.

[ix] Jerry L. Sumney, *Philippians: A Greek Students Intermediate Reader* (Peabody: Hendrickson Publishers, 2007), 39.

[x] http://www.nttext.org/commentary/entry/Phil.2.5 The HCNTTS textual commentary makes the point that "make" is active voice and "let" is passive.

[xi] Dole, *Hearts*, 110.

[xii] George A. Kennedy, *New Testament Interpretation Through Rhetorical Criticism* (Chapel Hill: University of North Carolina Press, 1984).

David W. Brown

Chapter 4

Mark 4:35 - 41
Commentary and Interpretation

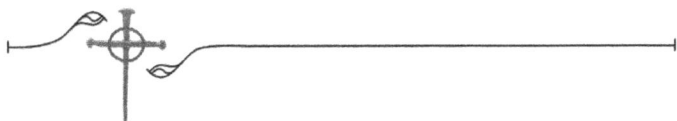

Great sermons are built by recognizing the questions that Scripture ask. This may sound somewhat ridiculous, but sometimes a story in the Scripture does not always give us a clear answer, and in this case, the question itself is vague. What does this passage teach believers? To find both the answer and a clear question in this passage, the pastor/teacher must look to the larger context.

This passage consists of a single paragraph and ends in verse forty-one with a question.[i] Actually, both verses forty and forty-one end with questions. Within the context, Mark records a conversation Jesus had with his disciples that begins and ends with similar wording in the Greek text:

* He says (legei)[ii] to them (4:35)
* He said (eipen) to them (4:40)

Jesus' question in verse forty is significant for our interpretation. "How is it that you have no faith?" The question of faith reflects a theme of faith in the larger context. Likewise, the question in verse forty-one is significant as well, and the answer is given in the larger context.

The current passage is a story that is located at the beginning of a series of five stories that all deal with a response of faith.[iii] The stories are structured as follows:

* Mark 4:35-41—Jesus exerts his authority over the wind and sea and responds in faith during difficult circumstances.

> * Mark 5:1-20—Jesus, by faith, casts out a legion of demons, restores a man to his right mind, and sends him out as a faithful follower.
> * Mark 5:24b-34—Jesus heals the woman with the hemorrhage who touches Jesus because of her faith in him.
> * Mark 5:21-25, 5:35-43—By faith, Jesus raises Jairus' daughter from the dead.
> * Mark 6:1-6 Jesus is unable to do any miracles in Nazareth because of their lack of faith.[iv]

Since repeated words and themes were a way of placing emphasis in ancient literature, this literary structure is important for the interpretation of the passage, since it begins a series of passages about faith. Jesus' question, "How is it that you have no faith?" is answered through this series of stories that all deal with a response by faith.

This leads us to the main point: if Jesus can calm storms, cast out a legion of demons, heal a woman with a hemorrhage, and raise someone from the dead, then the disciples should place their faith in him. Like the disciples, believers, are called to place our faith in Jesus as well. One important point should be noted here that deals with the last story of faith (Mark 6:1-6). The fact that Jesus did not perform any miracles is directly related to the lack of faith exhibited by the people of Nazareth.

The second question asked by the disciples is not only significant for interpretational purposes, but is intertwined with the question that deals with their faith. "Who is this, that even the wind and the sea obey him?" One of the major Christological titles associated with Jesus in Mark's Gospel is the "Son of God." This title is attributed to Him nine times in Mark's Gospel and seeks to answer the questions that are regularly asked that pertain to Jesus' identity.[v] The following verses emphasize the point:

> * 4:41–Who is this that controls the wind and the waves?
> * 6:2-3–Is this not the carpenter, the son of Mary... (i.e. who is this?)
> * 8:27–Who do people say that I am?
> * 8:29–Peter's dramatic confession "You are the Christ"

Despite the miracles performed by Jesus, the people fail to recognize who he truly is.[vi] Nonetheless, the readers of Mark's Gospel already know Jesus' identity because Mark has regularly told them that he is the "Son of

God."[vii] As a result, the disciples' failure to recognize Jesus' identity is the result of their lack of faith during the storm.[viii] In other words, the way believers are to build their faith in God is to recognize that Jesus is Lord and Savior. As the disciples slowly recognize Jesus' true identity, their faith begins to grow. Thus, the passage is not about Jesus calming the storms of our lives, but is rather a passage that teaches believers how to build their faith.

The first sub-point is that difficult circumstances will arise in life, and this sub-point is supported by verses thirty-six and thirty-seven. Contrast is important to recognize in this passage, and Mark emphasizes the ferocity of storm by contrasting it with the disciple's lack of faith. In this passage, fear is seen as the opposite of faith,[ix] and the description of Jesus peacefully sleeping on the cushion in the stern of the boat is a stark contrast to the raging storm.[x] Mark's objective becomes clear. He wrote the story for the expressed purpose to build the faith of the believer.

Problems will arise in life, and faith must be strengthened regularly in order to sustain the believer during the storms of life. Jesus' faith gave him the peace and security to sleep in the midst of a raging storm. In Psalm 4:8, the psalmist wrote, "In peace I will both lie down and sleep, for you alone, O' Lord, make me to dwell in safety." Faith gives believers the peace to endure the storms of life regardless of the difficulty of the storm.

The second sub-point Mark is making is that Jesus can help us through difficult circumstances, and this is supported by verses thirty-eight and thirty-nine. In response to the disciple's question, "Do you not care that we are perishing?" Jesus goes to great lengths to teach believers that he does care about their well-being. Jesus can deliver people from trials in life, but more importantly, Mark is emphasizing that rather than looking for miraculous deliverance from trials, it is far more important that believers build a solid faith in our Lord so they can endure the trials of life. Without trivializing the nature of difficult circumstances, Mark's objective is to build faith in the face of the difficulty at hand. To this extent, Jesus' sleeping during the storm is an indicator of his sovereignty in face of death.[xi] John Wayne once said, "Courage is being scared to death and saddling up anyway."[xii] Mark is making the same point in the passage. Sometimes, storms can be terribly frightening, but the mark of Christian maturity is a faith that is immoveable by the storms of life.

The final sub-point Mark makes in this passage is that Jesus challenges believers to build their faith in him, and this sub-point is supported by verse forty. Mark Guelich rightly points out the adverb "not yet" in verse forty suggests that something is lacking that could have or should have been expected.[xiii] From this perspective, Jesus' challenge to the disciples is to place their faith in him as Lord so they will not be found lacking. Faith in this context is not about holding correct doctrine, it is simply trusting that God will act through his son Jesus.[xiv]

Too often in Christian life, believers look for God to take them out of times of trials rather than allowing him to teach us how to persevere through trials and build our faith. As a result, we look for deliverance at the expense of spiritual growth, and this action plagues us for the rest of our lives. Hollywood is full of movies where the central character stares into the face of adversity and doesn't flinch, yet the reality is that believers not only fail to stare adversity in the face, we often run from it. This is a passage that calls believers to place our faith in Jesus and ask him to enable us to persevere through the trials of life.

Building Faith through the Storms of Life:
Stories of Faith in Mark's Gospel
Mark 4:35-41

INTRODUCTION:
Framing of the Passage:
> The passage consists of a single paragraph that is framed with two verbs from the same root (lego).
> * He says (legei) to them (4:35)
> * He said (eipen) to them (4:40)

Structure:
> The passage is located at the beginning of a series of five stories that all deal with a response to faith.
> * Mark 4:35-41 Jesus exerts his authority over the wind and sea and responds in faith during difficult circumstances.
> * Mark 5:1-20 Jesus casts out a legion of demons, restores a man to his right mind, and sends him out as a faithful follower.
> * Mark 5:24b-34 Jesus heals the woman with the hemorrhage who touches Jesus because of her faith in him.
> * Mark 5:21-25, 5:35-43 By faith, Jesus raises Jairus' daughter from the dead.
> * Mark 6:1-6 Jesus is unable to do any miracles in Nazareth because of their lack of faith.

Interpretational Thrust:
> Repeated themes place an emphasis on the context of the story and are directly related to Jesus' question, "How is it that you have no faith?"

The Problem:
> By failing to recognize who Jesus is (the Christ or Messiah), the disciples failed to place their faith in the one who could help them.

Main Point:
> If Jesus can calm storms, cast out a legion of demons, heal a woman with a hemorrhage, and raise someone from the dead, then the disciples should place their faith in him.

Application:
> Believers should place their faith in Jesus for any and all problems they deal with in life.

BODY
Sub-Points:
- I. **Difficult circumstances will arise in life (4:36-37).**
  - A) Difficult circumstances are bound to arise, but this does not mean we cannot have peace.
    - i. Note the contrast between the ferocity of the storm and the peace Jesus has while sleeping.
  - B) In this passage, fear is viewed as the opposite of faith.
    - i. The fact that the disciples had fear reflects they lacked faith.
  - C) Faith that cannot be sustained during the storms of life is a faith that is lacking God's peace and security and needs to be strengthened.
  - D) Psalm 4:8 "In peace I will both lie down and sleep, for you alone, O' Lord, make me to dwell in safety."
- II. **Jesus can help believers through difficult circumstances (4:38-39).**
  - A) In response to the disciples' question, "Do you not care we are perishing?" Jesus goes to great lengths to teach believers that he does care about our situations.
    - i. Jesus is not obtuse to the situation, but he is using the trial to strengthen the believer's faith.
  - B) Mark's objective is to build faith in the face of difficult circumstances, so the believer can have the faith Jesus exhibited by his sleeping during the storm.
    - i. John Wayne once said, "Courage is being scared to death and saddling up anyway."
- III. **Jesus challenges believers to build their faith upon him (4:40).**
  - A) The phrase "not yet" in verse forty suggest that something is lacking.
    - i. Lack of faith causes fear, which causes believers to turn away from Jesus.
    - ii. Mark teaches believers to build a faith in Jesus that can endure the storms of life.
  - B) Too often, believers look for God's deliverance rather than allowing God to teach us how to build our faith by persevering through the storms of life.

i. Rather than look for immediate deliverance, believers should attempt to understand what is lacking in our faith.

SUMMATION:
This is a passage that teaches believers to place their faith in Jesus in order to face the storms of life. The passage is not about Jesus calming the storms of our lives but is rather a passage that teaches believers how to build their faith in the midst of a storm in life. In order to do so, we recognize our Lord as the one to who can build our faith during the storms of life.

Final Thoughts:
In seminary life, students study a variety of subjects and are then tested in an effort to ensure they are grounded in their knowledge and understandings of that particular subject; in life, believers are tested through trials. In many ways, the typical evangelical church has failed to educate and instruct believers on the processes of building a faith that is grounded in doctrine, and like the disciples, believers today rush to Jesus with the same question, "Do you not care that we are perishing?" Trials in life can be frightening, and when our immediate petitions go unanswered, believers tragically turn their faith away from God.

This is a passage that seeks to build believers' faith in Jesus, who controls all things in life. At the same time, our desire for immediate responses to our prayers for deliverance from trials should not make us view God as obtuse, one who does not care about our circumstances. He is a sovereign God who is seeking to build believers' faith in him by teaching us to persevere through trials by placing our faith and trust in Jesus.

---

[i] Mounce, Basics, 13. In the Greek text a semicolon carries the same function as the English question mark.

[ii] Both (*legei*) and (*eipen*) are from the same root of (*lego*)

[iii] Fee and Stuart, *How to Read the Bible*, 282.

[iv] Ibid.

[v] The "Son of God" title is attributed to Jesus in 1:1, 1:11, 3:11, 5:7, 9:7, 12:6, 13:32, 14:64, and 15:39.

[vi] Burge, Cohick, Green, *The New Testament*, 182.

[vii] Luke Timothy Johnson, *The Writings of the New Testament*, 3rd ed. (Minneapolis: Fortress Press, 2010), 151.

[viii] Robert A. Guelich, "*Word Biblical Commentary Mark 1-8:26 vol. 34a*" (Grand Rapids: Thomas Nelson Publishing, 1989), 268.

[ix] Ben Witherington, *The Gospel of Mark: A Socio-Rhetorical Commentary* (Grand Rapids: William B. Eerdmans Publishing, 2001), 176-77.

[x] Ibid. 266.

[xi] Guelich, *Mark*, 266.

[xii] Dole, *Hearts*, 103.

[xiii] Guelich, *Mark*, 268.

[xiv] Rhoads, Dewey, Michie, "*Mark as Story*, 131.

Chapter 5

Matthew 26:36 - 56
Commentary and Interpretation

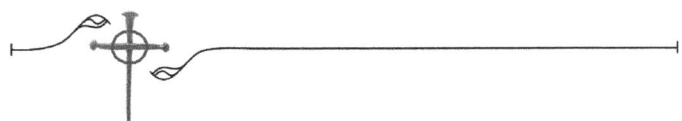

Great sermons come about by identifying sound hermeneutical principals within the Scripture that can be applied to the evangelical sermon and everyday life. Great sermons are sermons that teach solid theological doctrines of the Bible. They reveal the greatness of God's word to the congregation and inspire them to do great things.

This passage is a combination of three paragraphs that begin and end with similar wording and reflects progression.[i] The most recognizable feature in the passage is the prediction of the disciples' failure that leads to fulfillment of the Old Testament writings. This passage also reflects a common theme where a positive word or deed by Peter is followed by a reversal.[ii]

The larger context begins in verse thirty-one, and while this is important for interpretational purposes, it would be too large for practical purposes in a sermon presentation. Since the first paragraph highlights Jesus' prediction of the disciples' falling away, I would use this section in the introduction portion of the sermon as a means of building a setting. This would allow for proper time to reflect the contrasting faith in the passage, while the main portion of the sermon can be devoted to the disciples' falling away.

Nonetheless, the sermon passage (26:36-56) begins with Jesus coming into Gethsemane with his disciples (26:36) and ends with Jesus' arrest and his disciples abandoning him (26:56). This important literary feature is designed to reflect the same people encountering the same trial, but is contrasted with different responses and vastly diverse results. The primary literary feature can easily be seen as Jesus is regularly coupled together with his disciples. By continuing to place the disciples with Jesus, the numerous literary contrasts are easily recognizable:

* Then (*tote*) Jesus told them (the disciples) you will all fall away (26:31)
* Then (*tote*) Jesus came with them (the disciples) to a place (26:36)
* Then (*tote*) he (Jesus) came to the disciples (26:45)
* Then (*tote*) all the disciples left him (Jesus) fleeing (26:56)

Like the entrance and exit of a dramatic scene in a theatrical play, this type of literary feature frames the story about Jesus' faith. More importantly, the story contrasts Jesus' faith with the disciples' lack of faith. At the same time, the passage also parallels the disciples' spiritual abandonment with their physical abandonment. As they abandon their faith, they also abandon Jesus, who towers in his faith and endures the cross. The contrast between Jesus and the disciples is the central issue in this passage.[iii]

Jesus' faith is highlighted by the repetition of the verb "to pray" (*proseuchomai*) that appears five times in the first nine verses. By repeating the verb "to pray" over and over again, Matthew emphasizes Jesus' faith during one of the most significant trials of his life. Jesus' faith is contrasted by the disciples' lack of faith as they all fall asleep instead of pray. The constant repetition of contrasting faith between Jesus and his disciples can also be seen in Matthew's organization of verses thirty-six through forty-six. David Turner highlights the pattern describing them as a series of repeated cycles:

* Arrival in Gethsemane (26:36)
* The first cycle: Jesus prays and the disciples sleep (26:37-41)
* The second cycle: Jesus prays and the disciples sleep (26:42-43)
* The third cycle: Jesus prays and the disciples sleep (26:44-46)[iv]

Matthew highlights the contrast of faith by placing Jesus together with his disciples, yet as the faith of the disciples begins to fail, what emerges is a spatial distance between the two groups that parallels the spiritual differences emerging between them.[v]

The contrast between Jesus' faith and the faith of his disciples could not be more profound. In verse thirty-one, Jesus predicts the coming trial (his arrest) and the disciples falling away and being scattered. By contrast, the disciples not only fail to see the approaching trial but reject Jesus' prediction (26:33). In addition, Jesus yields his will to the Father's through prayer (26:42-43), and his faith is contrasted by the disciples failing to yield to Jesus' will as they all fall asleep (26:40, 43). Finally, Jesus' faith is sustained as he is arrested and goes to the cross (26:39, 42, 44) while the faith of the disciples fails them, and they are scattered (26:56).

The striking of the shepherd and scattering the sheep is a quote from Zechariah 13:7. Craig Blomberg maintained that the Zechariah passage coalesced around the figure of Jesus as a crucified Messiah, and this is precisely the context in which Jesus refers to the Scripture where the disciples are all scattered as he is arrested.[vi]

This leads to the main point of the passage: Jesus' faith is sustained through the trial because he prays and submits his will to the Father's. By contrast, the disciples fail to pray and submit their will to the Father, and as a result, their faith fails them. When Christians enter into times of trial, we should seek to sustain our faith through prayer and submission to the Father's will. If we choose not to follow Jesus' example, then our faith will fail us, just as the faith of the disciples failed them.

The first sub-point in the passage is the faithful believer should look for coming trials, and this is supported by verse thirty-eight. Trials in life sometimes catch Christians with our guard down because we do not have the spiritual maturity to see the trial coming. This aspect of spiritual insight is emphasized in verses thirty-eight and forty-one, where the disciples were commanded to keep watch. Matthew's emphasis to keep watch (*gregoreite*) is highlighted by the use of a present tense verb that denotes continuous action.[vii] An additional emphasis is made with the verb, since it is used in the imperative mood, which is used when making a command.[viii]

The point Matthew is emphasizing here is that faith that does not have the forbearance to look down the road of life is a faith that will be rocked by trial. The disciples were commanded on two different occasions to "keep watch" and failed. If believers cannot develop enough spiritual insight to listen to our Lord and anticipate coming trials when we are told in advance, our faith will fail us.

The second sub-point is that faithful believers pray in the midst of trials, and this is supported by verse thirty-nine.[ix] One of the key components in the spiritual success or failure of a believer is his/her ability to cope with trials. Immature Christians will typically come apart at the seams during times of trial, whereas the mature Christian will endure and persevere. The ironic part of this story is that both aspects are recorded in the passage as a means of placing contrast. Jesus anticipates the coming trial, prays, and submits his will to the Father. As a result, his faith is sustained through the trial and ultimately to the cross. Conversely, the disciples fail to see the coming trial, fall asleep rather than pray, and run away at Jesus' arrest. As a result, their faith is not sustained.

The cup Jesus mentions is commonly referred to by commentators as the cup of suffering and denotes the vicarious nature of Jesus' suffering.[x] His suffering is referred to metaphorically as a cup that must be drunk.[xi] In the midst of this anguish, Jesus submits his will to the Father's. The contrast between Jesus' suffering and the disciples sleeping cannot be more profound. Jesus commanded them to "keep watch" (26:41) and returned to find the opposite.[xii] If our faith is going persevere through difficult times, it will only be sustained by submitting our will to the Father's. Jesus' experience in Gethsemane is the example *par excellence*. Operatic soprano Beverly Sills made a pertinent point that applies to this type of situation when she said, "There are no shortcuts to any place worth going."[xiii] There are no shortcuts in faith. If believers are going to persevere through difficult times, we must have a faith that can sustain us.

The third sub-point is that faithful believers face their trials head-on, and this is supported by verses forty-five through forty-seven. The disciples have been commanded on two previous occasions to keep watch, and this somber warning is made evident in these three verses.[xiv] Matthew ominously notes the coming trial through a series of repeated interjections using the verb *idou*. Like a murder mystery whose killer is finally being revealed to the reader, Matthew slowly reveals Jesus' betrayer to his readers over the next three verses:

* Look (*idou*) the hour comes (26:45)
* Look (*idou*) my betrayer comes (26:46)
* Look (*idou*) Judas, one of the twelve, comes (26:47)

With the readers of Matthew's Gospel now on alert, Jesus commands his disciples to "get up go." Matthew's emphasis is noted by stacking two verbs together without the use of a conjunction to separate them.[xv] These literary and grammatical devices build to a climax where Jesus stands and faces his accusers head-on. Through prayer and submission to the Father's will, he is now strengthened to see God's work through to its conclusion.

As Jesus is speaking, Judas arrives with a crowd from the chief priest and the elders of the people carrying clubs and knives. The hypocrisy of Judas' actions can be seen in verse forty-nine as he refers to Jesus as rabbi, a title of respect, and kisses him, an action normally associated with brotherhood, affirmation, and honor.[xvi] Despite his betrayal and arrest, Jesus faces his trials with strength and fortitude, but at the same time, the disciples all scatter as Jesus is arrested. By falling asleep instead of praying and keeping watch as Jesus commanded them, they are ill-equipped to handle the trial, and their actions connote their lack of preparedness.

By recording this passage, Matthew presents a single trial that is received two very different ways. Jesus presents a model of how believers are to face trials in life. The disciples' running away reflects a model of what happens when believers are ill-prepared to face trials in life. Perseverance through trials can only be recognized through prayer and submission of the believers' will to our Father's.

David W. Brown

Trial, Prayer, and Submission:
Learning to Overcome Trials through Prayer and Submission
Matthew 26:36-56

INTRODUCTION:
Structure:
    The passage is a combination of three paragraphs that move from verse thirty-one to verse fifty-six. This is too large for a sermon presentation, but if the prophetic section is used as a type of introduction to the sermon, verses thirty-six through fifty-six can be used for the formal sermon.

Central Issue:
    The contrast between Jesus and the disciples is the central issue in this passage.

Literary Devices:
    The sermon passage begins (26:36) with Jesus coming into Gethsemane with his disciples and ends (26:56) with Jesus' arrest and His disciples abandoning Him.

Repetition and Emphasis:
    Jesus' faith is highlighted by the repetition of the verb "to pray" (*proseuchomai*) that appears five times in the first nine verses. By repeating the verb "to pray," Matthew emphasizes Jesus' faith during one of the most significant trials of his life. This repetition of faith is described as a series of repeated cycles:

    A. Arrival in Gethsemane (26:36)
    B. The first cycle: Jesus prays and the disciples sleep (26:37-41)
    C. The second cycle: Jesus prays and the disciples sleep (26:42-43)
    D. The third cycle: Jesus prays and the disciples sleep (26:44-46)

Main Point:
    Jesus' faith is sustained through the trial because he prays and submits his will to the Father's. Contrarily, the disciples fail to pray and submit their will to the Father, and as a result, their faith fails them.

Application:
When Christians enter into times of trial, they should seek to sustain their faith through prayer and submission to the Father's will.

BODY:
Sub-Points:
  I. **The faithful believer should look for coming trials (26:38).**
   A) The disciples are commanded to "keep watch" on two separate occasions (26:38, 41).
     i. Christians are sometimes blindsided by trials because we do not see them coming.
     ii. In the context, the disciples have already been warned of the coming trial (26:33) and have rejected Jesus' prediction.
     iii. Christians should heed the advice of their Christian mentors.
  II. **Faithful believers pray in the midst of trials (26:39).**
   A) One of the key components in the spiritual success of a believer is his/her ability to cope with the trial.
     i. Immature believers usually come apart at the seams, whereas mature believers persevere through trials.
   B) Jesus anticipates the coming trial because he heeds the advice of the Father, prays, and submits his will to the Father. As a result, his faith is sustained through the trial.
     i. By contrast, the disciples fail to see the coming trial, fall asleep rather than pray, and run away at Jesus' arrest. As a result, their faith is not sustained.
     ii. Operatic soprano Beverly Sills once said, "There are no shortcuts to any place worth going." This also pertains to faith.
  III. **Faithful believers face their trials head-on (26:45-47).**
   A) Matthew reveals his betrayer to be Judas to heighten the emphasis.
     i. Like a murder mystery whose killer is finally being revealed to the reader, Matthew slowly reveals Jesus' betrayer to his readers over the next three verses:

* Look (*idou*) the hour comes (26:45)
* Look (*idou*) my betrayer comes (26:46)
* Look (*idou*) Judas, one of the twelve, comes (26:47)

ii. These literary and grammatical devices build to a climax where Jesus stands and faces his accusers head-on.

SUMMATION:

Jesus presents a model of how believers are to face trials in life. Perseverance through trials can only be recognized through prayer and submission of the believer's will to our Father's.

Final Thoughts:

Literary structures play an important part of interpreting this passage and are important to note. By seeking the advice of our heavenly Father through prayer, believers can sustain our faith through trials.

---

[i] Walter C. Kaiser Jr., *Toward an Exegetical Theology: Biblical Principals for Preaching and Teaching* (Grand Rapids: Baker Books Publishing, 1981), 71-72.

[ii] Timothy Wiarda, *Interpreting Gospel Narratives: Scenes, People, and Theology* (Nashville: B&H Publishing Group, 2010), 180-187.

[iii] Grant R. Osborne, *Exegetical Commentary on the New Testament: Matthew* ed. Clinton E. Arnold (Grand Rapids: Zondervan Publishing, 2010), 971-72.

[iv] David L. Turner, *Baker Exegetical Commentary on the New Testament: Matthew* (Grand Rapids, Baker Academic Publishing, 2008), 632.

[v] This spatial and spiritual parallel can be seen following Jesus' arrest where Peter is described as following "at a distance" (26:58). As the spiritual distance grows so does the spatial distance. So, Peter follows first to the courtyard of the high priest (v58) and then ends with Peter standing in the gateway (even farther away) cursing and swearing that he does not know Jesus (v71).

[vi] Craig L. Blomberg, *Commentary on the New Testament Use of the Old Testament* ed. G. K. Beal and D. A. Carson (Grand Rapids, Baker Academic Publishing, 2007), 92.

[vii] Mounce, *Basics*, 310.

[viii] Ibid.

[ix] Jesus' praying is recorded three times in verses thirty-nine, forty-two, and forty-four and reflects sustained prayer for the full time he is in Gethsemane.

[x] Osborne, *Matthew*, 979.

[xi] Turner, *Matthew*, 631.

[xii] Mounce, *Basics*, 310. The present tense imperatives emphasize the on-going emphasis of "keeping watch" and "praying." This highlights the contrast all the more.

[xiii] Dole, *Hearts*, 113.

[xiv] Kaiser, *Exegetical Theology*, 71-72. Kaiser notes that specific patterns of progression are sometimes announced ahead of time in previous sections.

[xv] Andreas J. Köstenberger, Richard D. Patterson, *Invitation To Biblical Interpretation: Exploring the hermeneutical Triad of History, Literature, and Theology* (Grand Rapids: Kregal Academic & Professional Publishing, 2011), 592. An asyndeton form is one that is marked by the omission or absence of a conjunction between parts of a sentence.

[xvi] Turner, *Matthew*, 636.

David W. Brown

Sermons that use Parables

David W. Brown

Chapter 6

Luke 11:1 - 13
Commentary and Interpretation

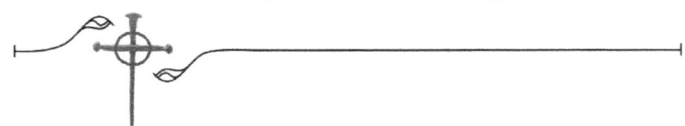

Great sermons teach believers the importance of a strong prayer life and persistence in asking for what we need. In this passage, Luke relays Jesus' example of good prayer and writes about the parable of the persistent traveler, which teaches us about the importance of prayer.

One of the most important aspects of building great sermons deals with how the biblical authors have organized the passage. Understanding the structure of a passage is crucial for interpretation, since meaning is found in the context of a passage.[i] There are two distinct paragraphs that make up this passage:[ii]

* Luke 11:1-4 deals with the concept of prayer
* Luke 11:5-13 deals with the parable of a persistent traveler[iii]

Noting where paragraphs begin and end is crucial for interpretation because paragraphs force the reader into understanding the passage in larger literary units than verse numbers do. For proper interpretation, I highly recommend to pastors/teachers to use an NASB or the ESV Bibles, since they follow the same paragraphs as the Greek New Testament. By coupling together these two paragraphs, Luke is emphasizing the idea of being persistent in our prayers.

In this passage, the context of the parable gives Luke's readers important clues that deal with the meaning he is trying to convey. This is a parable about prayer; more specifically, it is about the gift of prayer God gives the believer.[iv] The context of the parable describes Jesus praying in a particular place. After he had finished, his disciples came to him with a request for instruction on prayer:[v] "Teach us to pray just as John also taught his disciples" (11:1). This verse is crucial for interpretational purposes because not only does it supply the reader with the context of why the story is being told, it also teaches Luke's readers that this is going to be a passage that emphasizes boldness in our prayers.[vi]

To grasp Luke's emphasis in this passage about prayer, the preacher/teacher should build a general understanding about the New Testament authors.[vii] Because ancient Bibles did not have chapter divisions and verse numbers, readers in the ancient world read the Bible as a collection of stories.[viii] When the biblical authors wanted to emphasize specific aspects about a particular story, they used certain literary devices; namely the repeating of particular words, which rabbis called "pearl-stringing."[ix] Noting this literary device is crucial, since repetition has a cumulative type of effect that places an emphasis on understanding the larger context. The Greek word for prayer (*proseuchomai*) is repeated three times in the first two verses. In only two verses, Luke has both revealed the setting in the story and emphasized the concept of prayer by repeating this word multiple times. This leads us to our main point: Jesus calls believers to come boldly and persistently before our Lord to lay our prayers/petitions before him.[x] If a fallen human will respond to persistent asking, how much more will a holy God respond?[xi]

Social customs are also important in this passage because they contrast many of the modern conveniences we take for granted today.[xii] Conveniences such as cell phones, restaurants, hotels, and other "necessities" that all make journeys easier for the modern traveler did not exist in the ancient world. Today, when people travel to visit friends and relatives, they will typically call and let them know when they will be in town, but people in the ancient world did not have cell phones, and restaurants were limited. As a result, when people took trips, they would often show up unannounced and hungry. Unless preachers study these ancient biblical customs and educate their congregations, these social customs will go completely unnoticed by the average Christian sitting in service because modern interpreters have a tendency to read our present setting back into the Scripture.[xiii]

The first sub-point in the parable is that Jesus teaches believers how to pray, and this sub-point is emphasized in verses two through four.

Jesus begins the prayer by recognizing the Father, who is in Heaven. His thrust is that believers should recognize the one to whom we are voicing our prayers. Since God is in Heaven, and we are on earth, the idea teaches believers there is someone greater than ourselves, and believers should lay our prayers before the one who can help us. Our requests form an important part of our prayers, but they are not all of the prayer. God is not our personal genie waiting to grant our requests, and Christians should not treat him like one. Our prayers should not consist only of a list of requests we lay before our Lord. Another aspect of our prayer that Jesus taught deals with forgiveness. The NASB translates verse four as: "And forgive us our sins, for we forgive everyone who is indebted to us." Luke equates sin to a moral debt that fallen man has committed, and believers must seek our Lord's forgiveness.[xiv]

The second sub-point is that Luke teaches believers when to pray or how often to pray. Verses eight and nine support the notion of being persistent in our prayers, just as the midnight traveler was persistent in his request by continuing to knock. Some translations specifically use "persistence" in verse eight to describe the midnight traveler's attitude by continuing to knock on the friend's door. Although some translations use the word persistence, the word (*anaideian*) actually means shamelessness.[xv] The idea reflects the audacity of a shameless sinner who comes regularly before a holy God asking and seeking his presence and help. Luke uses this idea by referring to the shameless persistence of the traveler who continues to ask, seek, and knock at such a late hour. He does not give up!

At the beginning of the twentieth century, there was a charismatic preacher named Smith Wigglesworth who claimed that if a believer prayed to God more than six times about a particular issue, this reflected a lack of faith, and God would not answer that prayer.[xvi] The idea that God is going to set limits on the number of times the believer can go to Him in prayer is completely baseless. In this passage, the verbs translated as "ask," "seek," and "knock" are all present tense imperatives. Imperatives built on a present tense stem, such as those in verse nine, denote the continuous type of action,[xvii] of laying our prayers before God on a regular basis.

While the context in the parable emphasizes persistence in prayer, these Greek verbs reflect the idea of persistence as we go before our Lord, asking for and seeking his guidance throughout our prayers.

The persistency of the man in the parable is supported by grammar that indicates the believer should keep on asking, keep on seeking, and keep on knocking. In other words, do not give up! On the other hand, David Garland pointed out that prayer is not a spiritual crowbar or a jackhammer that pries open God's willingness to act, but rather a means by which Christians open themselves up to God, to grasp God's will and to be grasped by it.[xviii]

One other illustration is helpful as well. When someone knocks on a door of a friend's house, they do not knock only once. We typically knock several times, and if we do not get a response, we knock again. The same concept applies in the passage, since the Greek verb denotes an ongoing knocking.[xix] When we go to the Lord with our prayers/requests, we are commanded to bring them before Him on an on-going basis. The thrust Luke is making is that we are not going to wear God out, no matter how often we pray.

The third sub-point is that Jesus teaches believers what to ask for in our prayers. In verse thirteen, Luke equates the good gifts to the Holy Spirit.[xx] This is important for the reader to grasp because Luke is emphasizing what the believer should ask for in his/her prayer. I once heard a sermon preached in chapel at seminary where the professor told the story of a storm that had awakened his young son while sleeping.[xxi] His first attempt to bring comfort to his son was by giving him a toy and assuring him that everything was going to be all right. After a few minutes, the young boy soon drifted off to sleep, but at the next clap of thunder, the boy was awake once again. This routine continued until the father recognized that it was not things the boy desired, but his father's presence.

Luke is making the same point in the parable. Anybody can make it through the good days, but Luke is teaching believers that our Lord will help us make it through the bad days. When we enter into times of trial, more than anything else in life, we need the presence of our heavenly Father, and this is what we should ask him for. Things will not carry us through tough times in life, but the presence of our heavenly Father will. When Christians enter into difficult circumstances, Jesus calls us to come boldly before Him in prayer and ask for the greatest gift of all, the good gift in verse thirteen, and that is the gift of the presence of God.

Prayers, Midnight Travelers, and Good Gifts:
Luke's Parable About the Gift of Prayer
Luke 11:1-13

INTRODUCTION:
Setting:
"Lord, teach us to pray just as John also taught his disciples" (11:1b). The setting is one of prayer.

Structure:
The passage is broken down into two distinct parts:
* Luke 11:1-4 deals with the concept of prayer.
* Luke 11:5-13 deals with the parable of a persistent traveler.

Organizational Thrust:
By coupling together these two paragraphs, Luke emphasizes the importance of persistence in our prayers.

Main Point:
Jesus calls believers to come boldly before Him and to lay our prayers/petitions before our Lord.

BODY:
Sub-points:
I. Jesus teaches believers how to pray (11:2-4).
   A) Recognize our Holy Father as the one to whom we pray (11:2).
      i. Lay our requests/prayers before Him (11:3).
      ii. Ask God to forgive us where we have failed Him (11:4).
II. Jesus teaches believers when to pray or how often to pray (11:5-9).
   A) Be persistent in our prayers (11:8).
      i. We are not going to wear God out no matter how often we pray (11:9).
   B) Smith Wigglesworth (a preacher from the early twentieth century) said: "If you pray more than 6 times this reflects a lack of faith and God will not answer that prayer."
      i. In the original Greek the verbs ask, seek, and knock all denote a continuous type of action (11:9).

III. Jesus teaches believers what to ask for in our prayers (11:13).
  A. The good gifts are being equated to the Holy Spirit.
  B. Tell the story of the little boy who gets scared when a thunderstorm blows over his house:
   * The father runs down the hall to his son's room.
   * First time the father gives him a toy.
   * Last time the father gives him something to drink.
   * The point of the story is that it was not *things* that the little boy desired but the presence of his father.
   * Luke makes the same point for believers.
   * Anybody can make it through the good days.
   * Luke is teaching us that our heavenly Father will be with us even in the bad days.
   * It is not *things* that get us through the tough times in life, but rather the presence of our heavenly Father.

SUMMATION:
This is a parable about prayer and teaches us:

I.   How to pray
II. When to pray or how often to pray
III. What to ask for in our prayers

When we enter into difficult circumstances in life, Jesus calls us to come boldly before Him and ask for the greatest gift of all (the good gift in verse thirteen); the gift of the presence of God.

Final Thoughts:
In many ways, preaching sermons are similar to lawyers arguing over a specific point of a case. Passages cannot be interpreted any way we want; preachers must advocate a proper way to interpret a particular passage. It is crucial for the pastor to note setting, structure, organizational thrust, and the main point in sermons or teaching outlines. Each of these areas has a cumulative effect on a sermon that builds to a climax of orthodox understanding. Also, the main point should be repeated multiple times throughout the sermon in an effort to drive home this emphasis.

This passage emphasizes the gift of prayer that God has given the believer. Our Lord wants to hear from us on a regular basis throughout the day. Regardless of how small our prayers may seem to us, our heavenly Father commands believers to lay our petitions before him. Our Lord already knows our situation, and the only thing that is going to get us through difficult times is the gift of His presence. Our prayers should reflect His word as we enter into these difficult circumstances.

---

[i] Osborne, *Spiral*, 37-51.

[ii] Both the *Nestle-Aland Novum Testamentum Graece* 27th edition and the *United Bible Society's* 4th edition place paragraph markers at verses 1 and 5.

[iii] Verses 1, 5, and 14 all begin new paragraphs in the Greek New Testament.

[iv] Walter L. Liefeld, "Parables on Prayer" in *the Challenge of Jesus' Parables*: ed. Richard N. Longenecker, (Grand Rapids: William B. Eerdmans Publishing, 2000), 240-62.

[v] The Greek verb for "teach" is an imperative.

[vi] Klyne R. Snodgrass, *Stories with Intent: A Comprehensive Guide to the Parables of Jesus* (Grand Rapids: William B. Eerdmans Publishing, 2008), 448.

[vii] Harry Y. Gamble, *Books and Readers in the Early Church: A History of Early Christian Texts* (New Haven: Yale University Press, 1995). The text also discusses literacy rates in the ancient world.

[viii] Mark Allen Powell, *What is Narrative Criticism?* (Minneapolis: Augsburg Fortress, 1990), 2. See also *Mark as Story: Retrospect and Prospect*, ed. Kelly R. Iverson and Christopher W. Skinner (Atlanta: Society of Biblical Literature, 2011).

[ix] Osborne, *Spiral*, 52.

[x] Joseph A. Fiztmyer, *The Gospel According to Luke X-XXIV* (Garden City, Doubleday Publishing, 1985), 910.

[xi] Snodgrass, *Stories*, 441.

[xii] Bruce J. Malina, *Windows on the World of Jesus: Time Travel to Ancient Judea* (Louisville: Westminster John Knox Publishing, 1993).

[xiii] Hans W. Frei, *The Eclipse of Biblical Narrative: A Study in Eighteenth and Nineteenth Century Hermeneutics* (New Haven: Yale University Press, 1974), 51-65.

[xiv] Martin M. Culy, Mikeal C. Parsons, and Joshua J. Stigall, *Luke: A Handbook On The Greek Text* (Waco: Baylor University Press, 2010), 375.

[xv] W. Bauer, F.W. Danker, W.F. Arndt, and F. W. Gingrich, *Greek-English Lexicon of the New Testament and Other Early Christian Literature* (Chicago: University of Chicago Press, 2000), 63.

[xvi] Larry Keefauver, *Smith Wigglesworth on Faith* (Mary, FL, Charisma House Publishing, 1996), 47-48.

[xvii] Mounce, *Basics*, 315.

[xviii] David E. Garland, *Exegetical Commentary on the New Testament: Luke* ed. Clinton E. Arnold (Grand Rapids: Zondervan Publishing, 2011), 473.

[xix] Ibid.

[xx] Ibid., 456-75.

[xxi] Argile Smith, "Diminishing the Distance" in the *Theological Educator* No. 57 Spring 1998): 121-28.

Chapter 7

Luke 15:11 - 32
Commentary and Interpretation

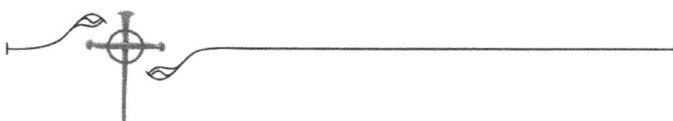

Great sermons teach that God alone saves those who are lost. One of the problems that plagues spiritual growth in evangelical church life is the view that believers are the focal point of the Christian faith, and this mindset is all the more difficult to break out of when Sunday School literature promotes this type of understanding.[i] This passage is a parable that emphasizes the greatness of God's love and forgiveness, and Luke goes to great lengths to teach believers that God seeks us, God finds us, and God saves us.

To come to a proper understanding of the passage, this parable must be interpreted along with the two previous parables in the larger context. Although the sermon itself will focus on the parable of the prodigal son, the larger context must include the parable of the lost sheep and the parable of the lost coin. There are a number of literary devices that support this rationale. First, all three parables tell the story of something lost that was later found. Second, the movement from animals, to objects, to people serves to emphasize the compassion God has for mankind; the rhetorical effect of placing three parables in a row climaxes at God's love for humanity and a proper response by man. Thus, a proper orthodox understanding for all three parables is that God seeks, finds, and saves what is lost.

In addition, Luke moves his readers to a progressively personal relationship between God and humanity by moving to smaller numerical units as he moves from parable to parable:

* 1 of 100 sheep (15:4)
* 1 of 10 coins (15:8)
* 1 of 2 sons (15:11)

These literary features are profoundly important from a doctrinal standpoint. One of the problems I have noticed in evangelical life during my years as a pastor is the emphasis that believers place on the profession of faith. I once served at a church where the same believers were being baptized repeatedly and their salvation (in their view) was determined by their own dogmatic certainty. Stephen Barton rightly asserted that these types of heretical fallacies are rooted in Enlightenment rationalism and a hermeneutic that perceives our own views as superior to those of the past.[ii]

Recognizing the repeated literary theme that God finds and saves what is lost in each of these parables is crucial because Luke is emphasizing that professions of faith do not center around the believer, but rather on a sovereign God who rejoices at saving what was once lost. If the emphasis were on the believer's profession, how would a sheep save itself? Better yet, how would a coin save itself?

Although the parable of the prodigal son consists of only two paragraphs, recognizing these literary devices in the parable are crucial for interpretation, because Luke is contrasting God's gracious salvation with the helpless state of mankind.[iii] Contrast is used throughout the parable to reflect the state of helplessness of the lost son. Kenneth Bailey reflected the contrasting imagery in a chiastic structure:[iv]

A) Death (15:12)
    B) All is Lost (15:14)
        C) Unqualified Rejection (15:15-16)
            D) The Problem (15:17)
            D) The Solution (15:18)
        C) Unqualified Acceptance (15:20)
    B) All is Found (15:22)
A) Life (15:24)

Seen in this format, the contrast is obvious and points to the helpless state of mankind and the dramatic reversal Jesus provides. By organizing the parable in this contrasting format, Luke leads the reader to the conclusion that mankind is helpless to save itself, but a rejoicing God mercifully saves us through his son. The main point of the parable is that God rejoices at finding and saving what was lost.[v] He recognizes the helpless state of humanity, and because of his great love for us, he seeks to bring mankind into a saving relationship with him.

An additional literary feature is that the parable is framed between the grumbling of the Pharisees (15:1-2) and the grumbling of elder brother (15:29-30). The hardness of the elder brother's heart parallels that of the Pharisees, while at the same time, contrasts the kindness of our Lord, who rejoices at saving what was once lost.[vi]

The first sub-point is the prodigal son was lost, and this is supported by verses twelve through sixteen. The state of the prodigal son is described from a literary perspective in these verses, so it is crucial the pastor/teacher recognize these descriptions and their implications. Four examples are listed below:

> * The request for his inheritance is another way of telling the father the prodigal wished he were dead (15:12)[vii]. The prodigal's request for his inheritance leads to the father's dividing his "wealth." The Greek text literally states the father divided his life.[viii]
> * The squandering of his estate is another way of describing financial destitution or no financial means (15:13).
> * The famine describes no food or physical means for survival (15:14).
> * The rejection by foreigners for the purpose of hiring himself out describes the prodigal's failure to even make a living (15:15).

All of these literary references have a cumulative type of effect that describes the lost state of the prodigal son. He had a broken relationship with his family, no money, no food, and no means to make a living. The helplessness of the situation reaches a new low in verse sixteen, where Luke describes a hungry Jewish boy longing for the food that animals would normally eat. The prodigal son had reached rock bottom.

The second sub-point is the prodigal son comes to his senses, and this is supported by verses seventeen and eighteen. Luke highlights the change in the prodigal's attitude in verse seventeen by stating that he came (*erchomai*) to his senses. Howard Marshall claimed this phrase is a Semitic way of talking about repentance.[ix] In addition, the verb (*poreuomai*) in verse eighteen is a movement verb that describes a swift and decisive attitude of repentance.[x] Both of these verbs have a cumulative type of effect that builds on the prodigal's helpless state and reaches a climax through the action of repentance.

A question that must be answered is how did the prodigal son sin against Heaven? Martin Culy, Mikeal Parsons, and Joshua Stigall all pointed out that the preposition "in the heavens," when used with sin (*hamartano*) in verse eighteen, indicates the sin is directed toward Heaven.[xi] The answer to this question, however, is found in Old Testament violations of the law, ranging from the request of his share of the possessions,[xii] his covetousness,[xiii] his leaving,[xiv] his squandering,[xv] and his lifestyle. As Klyne Snodgrass noted, the prodigal would have been guilty of violating the command in Exodus 20:12 to honor one's parents.[xvi] The point to all of this is that God rejoices when sinners recognize their helpless and lost situation and come to their senses by asking God to save them. This contrasting repetition that the dead have been brought to life and the lost have been found calls for rejoicing.[xvii]

This leads to the third sub-point, and that is God finds and saves what is lost, and this concept is supported by verses twenty through twenty-two. Contrasting themes abound in this parable and range from a God who finds being contrasted by what was once lost. Likewise, the starving prodigal who longs to eat the food that pigs were eating is contrasted with a loving father who kills the fatted calf to celebrate the restoration of his son. In addition, the elder son who grumbles at the return of the prodigal contrasts the rejoicing father. This is significant for interpretational purposes. The grumbling elder son reflects the grumbling of the Pharisees earlier in the chapter. The parallel attitudes between the Pharisees and the older brother are aligned for the purposes of equating the two in the parable.[xviii] Their grumbling frames the passage.

An additional contrast is described with a spatial comparison in verse twenty, where even though the prodigal was still a long way off, his father saw him and felt compassion for him. The spatial comparison reflects a holy God in Heaven who looks upon a broken relationship with man on earth (someone who is a long way off), and restores and saves the relationship. All of these contrasts are designed to lead the reader to recognize how radically different God's attitude is from that of man's, and therefore, believers are to join God in rejoicing at the work he has done.

GROUNDED: *Anchoring the Evangelical Sermon in Theological Doctrine*

In his book *Excellence*, Andreas Köstenberger drew the same contrast about his efforts in academic study. Like the prodigal son whose older brother grumbled about him, so Köstenberger has received the same grumbling for including faith in his academic pursuits. In his text, he pleads with zealous young theological students to incorporate this radical way of thinking into their theological endeavors and not to sacrifice their scholarly integrity for the sake of attaining academic respectability.[xix]

By turning our hearts and minds to the theological pursuit of living in this radical way, we as believers come to our senses and allow a rejoicing God to reach down from Heaven and save those who are lost. God's love is reflected in the fact that he rejoices at saving the lost.

David W. Brown

Lost Sheep, Lost Coins, and Lost Sons:
Three Parables Pointing to One Savior and His Work
Luke 15:11-32

INTRODUCTION:

Theological Emphasis:
 The greatness of God's love and forgiveness of mankind.

Theological Themes:
 The parable of the Prodigal Son consists of two paragraphs, and the parables of the Lost Sheep and the Lost Coin must also be included for interpretational purposes.
 1. All three parables emphasize something lost that was later found.
 2. The movement from animals, to objects, to people emphasizes God's love for humanity.
 3. Luke emphasizes the personal nature of God's relationship with humanity by moving to progressively smaller units:
    * 1 of 100 sheep (15:4)
    * 1 of 10 coins (15:8)
    * 1 of 2 sons (15:11)
 4. The passage is framed by the grumbling Pharisees and the grumbling elder brother.

Theological Thrust:
 The thrust found in each of these parables is that something that was once lost was later found.

Literary Devices:
 The parable is designed to reflect the dramatic reversal that Jesus provides repentant sinners and is reflected in a chiastic structure:

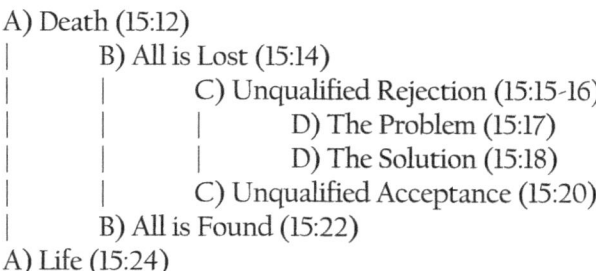

Main Point:
    God rejoices at saving what was once lost.

BODY:
Sub-Points:
    I. **The prodigal son was lost (15:12-16).**
        A) The lost state of mankind is exhibited by the prodigal and is reflected from a literary perspective in various ways:
            i. The request for his inheritance is another way of telling the father the prodigal wished he were dead (15:12).
            ii. The squandering of his estate is another way of describing financial destitution or no financial means (15:13).
            iii. The famine describes no food or physical means for survival (15:14).
            iv. The rejection by foreigners for the purpose of hiring himself out describes the prodigal's failure to even make a living (15:15).
        B) All of these literary references have a cumulative type of effect that describes the lost state of the prodigal son.
            i. He had a broken relationship with his family, no money, no food, and no means to make a living.
            ii. The helplessness of the situation reaches a new low in verse sixteen, where Luke describes a hungry Jewish boy longing for the food that animals would normally eat.
            iii. The prodigal son had reached rock bottom.
    II. **The prodigal son comes to his senses (15:17-18).**
        A) Luke notes the change in the prodigal's attitude.
            i. Coming to ones senses is Semitic language for talking about repentance.

      ii. The verb *erchomai* in verse seventeen is a movement verb that describes a swift and decisive attitude of repentance. Likewise, *poreuomai* in verse eighteen is typically translated as proceed and reflects proceeding from a state of helplessness to repentance.

      iii. These verbs have a cumulative type of effect that builds on the prodigal's helpless state and reach a climax through the action of repentance.

  B) The prodigal would have been guilty of violating the command in Exodus 20:12 to honor his parents.

  C) The point emphasized is that God rejoices when sinners recognize their helpless and lost situation and come to their senses by asking God to save them.

III. **God finds and saves what is lost (v20-22).**
  A) Notes the various contrasting points:
      i. A God who finds is being contrasted by what was once lost.
      ii. The starving prodigal is contrasted with a loving father who celebrates the restoration of his son.
      iii. The elder son grumbles at the return of the prodigal contrasts the rejoicing father.
      iv. The grumbling elder son reflects the grumbling of the Pharisees. The parallel attitudes are aligned for the purposes of equating the two in the parable, and their grumbling frames the passage.

  B) Note the spatial comparison:
      i. While the prodigal was a long way off, his father saw him and felt compassion for him.
      ii. The spatial comparison reflects a holy God in Heaven, who looks upon a broken relationship with man on earth (someone who is a long way off), and restores and saves the relationship.
      iii. All of these contrasts are designed to lead the reader to recognize how radically different God's attitude is from that of man's, and therefore, believers are to join God in rejoicing at the work he has done.

SUMMATION:

This is a parable that teaches that God rejoices at saving what was once lost. Jesus offers a radical reversal to repentant sinners who:

1. Forsake our sinful lives and comes to our senses
2. Ask God to save us

Final Thoughts:

This parable uses an enormous number of contrasts to emphasize the lost state of humanity and a loving God who rejoices at saving what was once lost. The congregation can only come to a proper orthodox understanding of this parable by bringing out the large number of contrasting examples. If proclaimed in this format, the congregation can begin to see how radically different God's way of thinking is truly different from that of sinful man's. Believers are not the center point of the Christian faith, and our focus should be our Lord Jesus who is the center point of our faith rather than focusing on ourselves.

---

[i] Unknown Author, *The Parables of Jesus: Understanding the Savior*, (Nashville: The Serendipity House, 2004), 19-20. In the Questions for Interaction section six of the eight questions emphasized the believers and their responses even though all three of the parables emphasize God seeks, God finds, and God saves.

[ii] Stephen C. Barton, "Parables on God's Love and Forgiveness" in *the Challenge of Jesus' Parables*: ed. Richard N. Longenecker, (Grand Rapids: William B. Eerdmans Publishing, 2000), 199-216.

[iii] Both the Nestle-Aland and the UBS reflect new paragraphs at verses eleven and twenty-five.

[iv] Kenneth E. Bailey, *Jacob & the Prodigal: How Jesus Retold Israel's Story* (Downers Grove: InterVarsity Press, 2003), 96.

[v] Craig L. Blomberg, *Interpreting the Parables* (Downers Grove: InterVarsity Press, 1990), 172-73.

[vi] Snodgrass, *Stories*, 95.

[vii] Kenneth E. Bailey, *Poet and the Peasant: A Literary-Cultural Approach to the Parables in Luke* (Grand Rapids: William B. Eerdmans Publishing, 1976), 161.

[viii] The Greek word for wealth is the word *bios*.

[ix] I. Howard Marshall, *The New International Greek New Testament Commentary: The Gospel of Luke* (Grand Rapids: William B. Eerdmans Publishing, 1978), 609.

[x] Ibid.

[xi] Culy, Parsons, Stigall, *Luke*, 508.

[xii] Bailey, *Poet*, 161-62

[xiii] David A. Holgate, *Prodigality, Liberality and Meanness: The Prodigal Son in Greco-Roman Perspective* (Sheffield: Sheffield Academic, 1999) 208.

[xiv] Herman Hendrickx, "A Man Had Two Sons: Lk. 15:11-32 in Light of the Ancient Mediterranean Values of Farming and Household." *East Asian Pastoral Institute* 31 (1994): 44-66.

[xv] François Bovon, "The Parable of the Prodigal Son (Luke 15:11-32):) First Reading," in *Exegesis: Problems of Method and Exercises in Reading (Genesis 22 and Luke 15)* (ed. François Bovon and Gregoire Rouiller; trans. Donald G. Miller, Pittsburgh; Pickwick, 1978), pp. 43-73, see p. 53; Donahue, The Gospel in the Parable, p. 154.

[xvi] Snodgrass, *Stories*, 131.

[xvii] Garland, *Luke*, 633.

[xviii] Craig S. Keener, *The IVP Bible Background Commentary: New Testament* (Downers Grove, InterVarsity Press, 1993), 233-34.

[xix] Andreas J. Köstenburger, *Excellence: The Character of God and the Pursuit of Scholarly Virtue* (Wheaton: Crossway Publishing, 2011), 24.

Chapter 8

Mark 4:3 - 25
Commentary and Interpretation

Great sermons teach people how to better listen and understand the Word of God. Great sermons teach believers the importance of both discipleship and understanding Scripture. Following the deaths of the apostles, Christians no longer had eyewitness accounts of the stories of Jesus, and so the preeminence of listening to God's Word became the focal point of the Christian faith.[i] Great sermons emphasize God's Word as that focal point.

One of the most complex parables in Mark's Gospel is the parable of the soils. This parable spans four paragraphs in length and is regularly misinterpreted among Christians, primarily because we miss the literary devices built into the text. Some Christians have claimed this passage was a parable about true and false conversions, but this view is highly improbable.[ii] Advocates of this view see the good soil as the Christians and the other soils as non-Christians. The problem with this view is that the parable does not emphasize Christian conversions or making a profession of faith. In addition, this view is inherently problematic, as there is a tendency to portray the Christian faith as a sort of spiritual on/off switch that obliterates the concept of spiritual growth and discipleship.

By contrast, this is a parable about listening to God, and it emphasizes the spiritual barriers that stand in the way of true discipleship and Christian growth.[iii] There are several literary devices that support the notion about hearing. First, the parable begins (4:3) and ends (4:9) with the Greek command "to hear" (*akouo*). Bible students sometimes miss the repeated use of this word because some English Bibles translate the word (*akouo*)[iv] as "listen" rather than "hear." Second, the word *akouo* appears in various grammatical forms twelve times in the first twenty-five verses of the chapter. The word "to hear" not only frames the passage but is also mentioned in virtually every other verse, and this places a clear emphasis on the need to hear or to listen to God. Finally, Jesus' teaching in parables reveals the mystery of the Kingdom of God to the disciples and those on the inside. The insiders and outsiders motif is noted in a spatial reference to Jesus entering into the boat (an insider) and those on the land by the sea (outsiders).[v] Those on the inside are ones with eyes that see, ears that hear, and hearts that understand. In addition, Mark quotes Isaiah (4:10-12) where God commissioned the prophet for the expressed purpose of blinding the eyes and deafening the ears of the opposition (those on the outside).[vi]

The structure of the passage spans four paragraphs and appears in the following format:

* The parable of the soils (4:3-9)
* The quoting of Isaiah (4:10-12)
* The explanation for the parable (4:13-20)
* The explanation of the explanation (4:21-25)

The parable's structure is important for interpretational purposes, since the parable itself uses metaphorical descriptions that are explained in the paragraphs that follow. While the explanation for the parable is located in verses thirteen through twenty, all three paragraphs that follow the parable (verses 3-9) illuminate the need to listen to God.

Ched Meyers rightly argued the first three soils reflect obstacles to true discipleship and that each obstacle is followed with an example.[vii] Only the last soil speaks of those who welcome God's word and are obedient to it. The obstacles and their examples can be seen below:

* **Obstacle 1:** Satan, whose opposition ensures that potential disciples will remain "by the way" (4:15)
* **Example 1:** The crowd only listens but does not follow
* **Obstacle 2:** Tribulations and persecutions (4:17)
* **Example 2:** Disciples for whom suffering is a stumbling block
* **Obstacle 3:** Worries of this age, lure of wealth, and all other passions (4:19)
* **Example 3:** Discipleship rejection-such as the rich, young ruler[viii]

In verse nine, the parable of the soils finishes with the phrase "the one who has an ear to hear, let him hear," which teaches this parable is not for just anyone, but for only those with ears who have the ability to hear and listen to what God is saying.[ix] Greg Beale rightly argued that symbolic parables, like the parable of the soils, cause those who have ears to hear, to hear and understand, and those on the outside, who do not hear, to misunderstand further.[x]

This leads to the main point of the parable: true discipleship comes from listening to God and being obedient to his will. If the apostles were going to become truly devoted to Jesus, they must do something Israel had struggled with since the time of Isaiah; they must learn to listen to their Lord.

The first sub-point is true discipleship begins with listening to God, and this is supported in verses three and nine. Listening to God is not a theme unique to Mark's Gospel and the New Testament; it is intertwined throughout the Old Testament as well. In a 1985 article, Craig Evans rightly asserted that the concept of hearing God is firmly rooted in the Hebrew Scriptures and specifically the Deuteronomic Law.[xi] He suggested the parable was a Markan Midrash.[xii] He cited two examples:

* Deuteronomy 6:5, in which the three types of soils represent the struggle to love Yahweh with all of one's heart, soul, and might.
* Isaiah 55:10 asserts that Yahweh's word goes out but does not return void.

The focal point of Mark's parable is the emphasis that true discipleship begins with listening to God, which goes far beyond a simple profession of faith. True discipleship consists of a steady diet of listening to God through the study of his Word. This point is emphasized by Mark's repetitive use of three verbs "to hear" in a present tense form as seen below:

* "Listen/hear (*akouo*) [and] perceive the sower goes out to sow" (4:3)
* "And he said the one having ears to hear (*akouo*) let him hear (*akouo*)" (4:9)

In addition to using the present tense in all three verbs, two of the three verbs appear in an imperative form. As mentioned in previous passages, imperatives built on a present tense stem denote continuous action.[xiii] Mark is describing the on-going action of listening to God.

The second sub-point is true discipleship overcomes the stumbling blocks of life, and this is supported by verses fourteen through twenty. These verses all describe spiritual barriers to true discipleship. The obstacles and their examples have already been noted, but the thrust Mark is making in these verses is noted by the contrast between the unproductive soils and the good soil that produces phenomenal growth. His point is that hearing must be followed with action, and this is noted by the shift from the aorist tense verbs "to hear" that are used in verses fourteen through nineteen. However, beginning in verse twenty, the goods soil hears the word, receives it, and bears fruit. All of these verbs in verse twenty denote hearing, receiving, and bearing fruit in a present tense form that describes an on-going type of action. Mark is emphasizing the concept of listening to God, then growing and bearing fruit on a regular basis. God wants believers to work at bearing fruit on an on-going basis.

In pastoral life, there is a tendency for pastors/teachers to sometimes see themselves in a much more flattering light than what we should, and this struggle is often greater when we have a few theological degrees under our belt. We often view spiritual stumbling blocks as chains that only hinder those in the congregation with less education and less spiritual insight. But spiritual stumbling blocks emerge in pastoral life as items that make us comfortable. In many ways, they paralyze our spiritual growth by making us lazy and keep us from pushing ourselves to deeper understandings of God's word through theological study. I like what operatic soprano Beverly Sills once said, "You may be disappointed if you fail, but you are doomed if you don't try."[xiv] True discipleship calls us to overcome the stumbling blocks of Christian mediocrity.

The third sub-point is that God's Word will illuminate true discipleship and this is supported by verses twenty-one through twenty-three. Mark has already given an explanation (verses thirteen through twenty) to the parable. Now, he gives an explanation of the explanation. Meyers articulated this repetitive word play in verses twenty-one through twenty-two.[xv] The repetition is noted below.

* Nothing is hidden (*krupton*) (4:21)
    except what is made apparent (*phanerothe*) (4:21)
* Nor has anything been secreted (*apokrupton*) (4:22)
    except to be made apparent (*phaneron*) (4:22)

Mark closes the analogy by repeating the word "to listen" (*akouo*) in a present tense form. The word to hear/to listen is used in an imperative form, so the analogy closes with the command to listen continually.[xvi] Mark's repetitive word play illuminates the meaning of the parable.

Parables are sometimes characterized as earthly stories with heavenly meanings, but Meyers rightly argues this is exactly what they are not.[xvii] Meyers continued on to say that "parables are not enshrined in arcane knowledge, but rather, Mark grounds this parable in earthly/concrete meaning. They are not to be misconstrued as a lamp being concealed, but rather as a teaching meant to be illuminated." Parables were never designed to simply fill the reader with a secret knowledge of the Bible; they were designed to illuminate God's Word in order to help the listener to grasp what Jesus was emphasizing.

David W. Brown

True Discipleship and Israel's Failure to Listen: Mark's Parable of the Soils
Mark 4:1-25

INTRODUCTION:

Emphasis:

This is a parable about hearing God, and it emphasizes the spiritual barriers that stand in the way of true discipleship and Christian growth.

Literary Devices:

There are several literary devices that support the notion about hearing:
* The parable begins (4:3) and ends (4:9) with the Greek command "to hear" (*akouo*).
* The word (*akouo*) appears in various grammatical derivations twelve times in the first twenty-five verses. The verb "to hear" frames the passage.
* Mark's record of Jesus' teaching in parables reveals the mystery of the Kingdom of God to the disciples.

The Structure of the Parable:

The structure of the passage spans four paragraphs and appears in the following format:
* The parable of the soils (4:3-9)
* The quoting of Isaiah (4:10-12)
* The explanation for the parable (4:13-20)
* The explanation of the explanation (4:21-25)

Obstacles to True Discipleship:
* **Obstacle 1:** Satan, whose opposition ensures that potential disciples will remain "by the way" (4:15).
* **Example 1:** The crowd only listens but does not follow.
* **Obstacle 2:** Tribulations and persecutions (4:17).
* **Example 2:** Disciples for whom suffering is a stumbling block.

* **Obstacle 3:** Worries of this age, lure of wealth, and all other passions (4:19).
* **Example 3:** Discipleship rejection—such as the rich young ruler.

Main Point:
True discipleship comes from listening to God and being obedient to his will.

BODY:
Sub-Points:
I. **True discipleship begins with listening to God (4:3, 9).**
   A) Listening to God is not a theme unique to Mark's Gospel and the New Testament; it is intertwined throughout the Old Testament as well.
   Old Testament
   i. Deuteronomy 6:5 views the three types of soils representing the struggle to love Yahweh with all of one's heart, soul, and might.
   ii. Isaiah 55:10 asserts that Yahweh's word goes out but does not return void.
   iii. The point is that true discipleship begins by listening to Yahweh.
   New Testament
   i. The focal point to Mark's parable is the emphasis that true discipleship begins with listening to God.
   ii. Mark's repetitive use of three verbs "to hear" in a present tense form is seen below:
      * "Listen/hear (*akouo*) [and] perceive the sower goes out to sow" (4:3)
      * "And he said the one having ears to hear (akouo) let him hear (*akouo*)" (4:9)
II. **True discipleship overcomes the stumbling blocks of life (4:14-20).**
   A) The thrust Mark is making in these verses is noted in the contrast between the unproductive soils and the good soil that produces phenomenal growth.
   i. Hearing must be followed with action, and this is noted by the shift from the aorist tense (4:14) to the present tense (4:20).

  ii. Beginning in verse twenty, the goods soil hears the word, receives it, and bears fruit.
  iii. All of these verbs in verse twenty denote hearing, receiving, and bearing fruit in a present tense form that describes an on-going type of action.
  iv. Mark is emphasizing the concept of listening to God, then growing and bearing fruit on a regular basis.
III. God's Word will illuminate true discipleship (4:21-23).
 A) Note the repetitive word play:
  i. Nothing is hidden (*krupton*) (4:21) except what is made apparent (*phanerothe*).
  ii. Nor has anything been secreted (*apokrupton*) (4:22) except to be made apparent (*phaneron*).
 B) Mark closes the analogy by repeating the word "to listen" (*akouo*) in a present tense form.
  i. The word to hear/listen is used in an imperative form.
  ii. The analogy closes with the command to listen continually.

SUMMATION:

Parables are often characterized as earthly stories with heavenly meanings, but according to Meyers, this is exactly what they are not. Parables are not enshrined in arcane knowledge; Mark grounds this parable in earthly/concrete meaning. True discipleship comes from listening to God and being obedient to his will.

Final Thoughts:

Congregations will never be enlightened with dumbed-down sermons and teachings that lack depth. Disciples will only grow to spiritual maturity and be prepared to overcome the spiritual stumbling blocks in life by teaching deeper understandings of God's Word. Pastors/teachers are called to illuminate the teachings of God's Word through solid exegesis and proclaim them in a sermonic form found in expository preaching/teaching. The parable of the soils is a parable that places an emphasis on listening to God.

[i] Baukham, *Jesus and the Eye Witnesses*, 12-38.

[ii] Ray Comfort, *The Way of the Master*, (Orlando: Bridge Logos Publishing, 2006), 16. In his illustration Comfort uses Judas as the pinnacle of false conversions.

[iii] Ched Meyers, *Binding the Strong Man: A Political Reading of Mark's Story of Jesus - Anniversary Edition* (Maryknoll: Orbis Books Publishing, 2011), 175.

[iv] Mounce, *Basics*, 310. In the Greek language the imperative mood is used when making a command.

[v] Meyers, *Binding*, 174.

[vi] Fee and Stuart, *How to Read the Bible*, 281.

[vii] Meyers, *Binding*, 174-75.

[viii] Ibid.

[ix] Robert A. Guelich, *Word Biblical Commentary Mark 1-8:26* (Nashville: Thomas Nelson Publishing, 1989), 196.

[x] G.K. Beale, *The New International Greek Testament Commentary: Revelation* (Grand Rapids: William B. Eerdmans Publishing, 1999), 236-39. While Beale's commentary was written for the book of Revelation, the same methodology can be applied to this parable.

[xi] Craig Evans, "On the Isaianic Background of the Sower Parable" in *Catholic Biblical Quarterly*, 47, 464ff.

[xii] A Midrash was a commentary produced by Jewish rabbi's from the time of the Babylonian exile to approximately A.D. 1200.

[xiii] Mounce, *Basics*, 315.

[xiv] Dole, *Hearts*, 21.

[xv] Meyers, *Binding*, 176.

[xvi] Mounce, *Basics*, 315.

[xvii] Meyers, *Binding*, 173.

David W. Brown

Chapter 9

Matthew 25:1 - 13
Commentary and Interpretation

Great sermons teach believers what it means to be ready for the return of our Lord. They teach believers to live in a regular state of watchfulness rather than a state of panic. This is a parable in which its emphasis is revealed through a comparison. Like the earlier passage from Hebrews 5:11-6:12, this parable has a chapter division that falls in the middle of the passage.[i] The location of this chapter division greatly impacts the interpretation of this passage, since some Christians do not recognize the parable of the ten bridesmaids as part of a larger context.[ii]

Although the parable only spans thirteen verses, there is clear linguistic evidence that these paragraphs should be interpreted with the larger context, which includes the two preceding paragraphs from Matthew 24:42-51. The parable in its larger context (24:42-25:13) spans three paragraphs, but there can be little doubt that all three were meant to be interpreted together. Several literary features, listed below, reflect the striking similarities:

> * In the larger context, the passage begins (24:42) and ends (25:13) with the command to be ready (*gregoreite*).[iii]
> * In the larger context, both 24:44 and 25:10 advocate the concept of readiness by using the same word (*hetoimos*).[iv]
> * In the larger context, both 24:50 and 25:13 teach of an unknown day and hour that people are to be ready for.[v]

These literary features not only show that these three paragraphs should be interpreted together, but also have a cumulative type of effect that emphasizes the theme of being ready. Readiness, however, is not determined by calculating a date, but rather by how we are presently living.[vi] R. T. France rightly claimed that the parables in Matthew chapter twenty-five are all designed for a specific function. He wrote:

> There can be little doubt, therefore, of the intended application of these parables at the point where they occur in Matthew's Gospel. For Jesus—having "gone away" in his death, resurrection, and ascension to Heaven—will one day come back. But no one knows when that will be. His disciples must therefore be ready at all times. If they are not, there is the prospect of judgment.[vii]

While this parable emphasizes readiness, it does so through the use of allegorical imagery that pertains to Jewish customs concerning marriage.[viii] The parable compares readiness to participate in the celebration of a wedding to readiness to participate in the coming kingdom.[ix] According to Arland Hultgren, Jewish marriages were organized in two parts. The first was a betrothal stage, which was a contractual stage where the husband and wife were officially married.[x] The second stage was the celebration of the marriage, which is reflected by the bridesmaids attending the wedding.[xi]

The parable uses allegory to describe the Son of Man as the bridegroom, while the bridesmaids are the members of the messianic community, the church.[xii] The central thrust of the parable centers on the delay of the bridegroom and the readiness of the bridesmaids; the five who were not ready were not included in the wedding celebration.[xiii] The main point of the passage is that God calls his church to be ready for his return, even though we do not know when that will be.

The first sub-point is that God may delay his coming longer than people expect, and this is supported by verse five.[xiv] Matthew emphasizes the delay of the bridegroom by the use of a present tense participle for the word "delaying." Present tense participles denote an on-going type of action, so Matthew is describing a long delay.[xv] The Greek word translated as "delay" is from the root *chronos*. Our English word chronology comes from this word. The long delay Matthew is describing refers to the long delay the church has experienced and is still currently experiencing. This idea applies even to the apostles, who were looking for Jesus to return during their own lifetime. Since Matthew's Gospel was most likely written in the middle eighties[xvi] of the first century, Matthew himself was experiencing the same delay.

The second sub-point is that Jesus' followers must be ready for a delay, and this is supported by verses six through nine. Waiting on God can sometimes be difficult, but in this case, the delay has a purpose, and that is to differentiate the wise bridesmaids from the foolish ones. Grant Osborne makes the point that the cry is at the heart of the story and corresponds to the arrival (*Parousia*) of the bridegroom and begs the question "Who is ready to meet the bridegroom?"[xvii] The bridesmaids all rose and began to trim their lamps. According to Grant Osborne, the Greek verb for trimmed (*ekosmesan*) is an ingressive aorist and literally means "to adorn" or "to make ready."[xviii] In the context of the parable, it means to make the torches ready by putting on extra oil or replacing the burnt rags with new ones.[xix] The point that must be recognized is the wise bridesmaids were ready for the delay, and the foolish were not. France rightly stated:

> The unsuccessful attempt of the foolish girls to borrow from the wise may be no more than dramatic storytelling. But the moral would easily be drawn that "readiness" is something for which we are each responsible-that is, that we cannot be passengers on another person's readiness.[xx]

The third sub-point is those who are not ready for the return will face consequences, and this is supported by verses ten through thirteen. The turning point of the story comes when the door is ominously shut. At this point, the foolish bridesmaids, who were not ready, have returned from purchasing oil and are refused entry into the wedding celebration. The foolish bridesmaids had missed the return of the bridegroom while they were off purchasing additional oil they had failed to bring with them. There is a verse from Proverbs 13:9[xxi] that fits the ominous ending in the parable. "The light of the righteous shines brightly, but the lamp of the wicked is snuffed out." The point Matthew is emphasizing here is that failure to be ready for the Lord's return carries consequences.

At the opposite end of the spectrum were the wise bridesmaids, who were ready for the bridegroom. One of my professors in seminary had previously served for several years as a missionary to Columbia, and he emphasized that the people there operated by what he termed as "people time." Every Sunday morning prior to church, he would drive through the village honking the horn of the car to let everyone know the pastor was on his way to the church. He stressed, however, that church did not begin until all the right people had arrived. There was a woman in their village who, he claimed, was a sort of matriarch of the town, and the service did not begin until she had arrived. This was "people time," and this is what Matthew is describing in the story.[xxii] The right people are the wise bridesmaids who were ready for the bridegroom.

Readiness is not living in a state of red alert, but it is living characterized by believers who are regularly looking for our Lord's return. One of the most famous stories in American history is the notorious story of William Miller.[xxiii] Miller was a Baptist minister and a deist who had converted to the Christian faith. He believed that Christ was going to return to earth on March 21, 1843. He had arrived at this conclusion based upon a mathematical calculation he had created using the book of Daniel.

About a decade prior to Miller's predicted date, he began to preach about Jesus' return and by 1843 had amassed an enormous following.[xxiv] To make matters worse, Miller had cast himself and his followers as the five wise virgins of Matthew 25:1-13. On March 20, 1843 Miller and his followers donned their ascension robes, and some even climbed trees in anticipation of the Lord's return. The climbing of trees would in fact shorten the distance between Heaven and earth and, no doubt, speed the process of going to Heaven.

Unfortunately for Miller and his followers, March 21, 1843 came and went without the Lord's return. The aftermath of what came to be known as *the Great Disappointment* and was far worse than what anyone could have imagined.[xxv] The cold winter of 1844-45 lay ahead, and some had failed to provide for their needs. However, Stephen O'Leary pointed out that the experience of physical hunger paled in comparison to the spiritual deprivation that Miller and his followers had experienced following the debacle.[xxvi] One of his followers later wrote:

> Our fondest hopes and expectations were blasted, and such a spirit of weeping came over us as I had never experienced before. It seemed that the loss of all earthly friends could have been no comparison. We wept until the day dawn.[xxvii]

Matthew's command to be ready does not call believers to live in a state of red alert but to live a life characterized by watchfulness reflected by the believer's spiritual understanding of the Bible. Christians rise or fall based upon their relationship with God through their understanding of his Word. Failure to grasp the spiritual significance of his Word and to prepare for his return leads to judgment.

David W. Brown

Parable, Metaphor, and Readiness:
Are we Prepared for the Coming of our Lord?
Matthew 25:1-13

INTRODUCTION:
Structure:
> The parable in its larger context (24:42-25:13) spans three paragraphs, but all are meant to be interpreted together.
> * In the larger context, the passage begins (24:42) and ends (25:13) with the command to be ready (*gregoreite*).
> * In the larger context, both 24:44 and 25:10 advocate the concept of readiness by using the same word (*hetoimos*).
> * In the larger context, both 24:50 and 25:13 teach of an unknown day and hour that people are to be ready for.

Allegorical Comparison:
> The parable uses allegory to describe the Son of Man as the bridegroom and the members of the messianic community, the church, as the bridesmaids. It compares readiness to participate in the celebration of a wedding to readiness to participate in the coming kingdom.

Central Thrust:
> The central thrust of the parable centers on the delay of the bridegroom and the readiness of the bridesmaids; the five who were not ready were not included in the wedding celebration.

Main Point:
> The main point is that God calls his church to be ready for his return, even though we do not know when that will be.

BODY:
Sub-Points:
> I. God may delay his coming longer than people expect (25:5).
>> A) Matthew emphasizes the delay of the bridegroom by the use of a present tense participle for the word "delaying."

i. Present tense participles denote an on-going type of action, so Matthew is describing a long delay.
ii. The Greek word translated delay is from the root *chronos*.
iii. Our English word chronology comes from this word.
iv. The long delay Matthew is describing refers to the long delay the church has experienced and is still currently experiencing.

II. **Jesus' followers must be ready for a delay (25:6-9).**
   A) The delay has a purpose, and that is to differentiate the wise bridesmaids from the foolish ones.
      i. The purpose asks a rhetorical question "Who is ready to meet the bridegroom?"
   B) The Greek verb for "trimmed" (*ekosmesan*) literally means "to adorn" or "to make ready."
      i. In the context of the parable, it means to make the torches ready by putting on extra oil or replacing the burnt rags with new ones.
      ii. The point that must be recognized is the wise bridesmaids were ready for the delay, and the foolish were not.

III. **Those who are not ready for the return will face consequences (25:10-13).**
   A) Note the contrast from those who were ready to those who were not:

   Those who were ready:
      i. One of my professors in seminary had previously served for several years as a missionary to Columbia and he emphasized that the people there operated by what he termed as "people time."
      ii. Every Sunday morning prior to church, he would drive through the village blowing the horn of the car to let everyone know the pastor was on his way to the church.
      iii. He stressed, however, that church did not begin until all the right people had arrived.
      iv. There was a woman in their village who, he claimed, was a sort of matriarch of the town, and services did not begin until she had arrived.
      v. This was "people time," and this is what Matthew is describing in the story.

            vi. The right people are the wise bridesmaids who were ready for the bridegroom.
         Those who were not ready:
            i. At the opposite end of the spectrum were the foolish bridesmaids who had missed the return of the bridegroom while they were off purchasing additional oil they had failed to bring with them.
            ii. Proverbs 13:9 "The light of the righteous shines brightly, but the lamp of the wicked is snuffed out."
            iii. The point Matthew is emphasizing is that failure to be ready for the Lord's return carries consequences.
      B. Readiness is not living in a state of red alert.
            i. Tell the story of William Miller and his followers (see commentary).

SUMMATION:
God calls his church to be ready for his return, even though we do not know when that will be. Matthew's command to be ready does not call believers to live in a state of red alert, but to live a life characterized by vigilance and anticipation for his return.

Final Thoughts:
One of the most damaging views evangelicals hold is that while we may not know the exact date of the Lord's return, we can know the general time frame. Since Jesus himself said he did not know when this day will come, the idea that we might know reaches the height of man's arrogance. The truth of the matter is that nobody knows, and this parable and the parable of the talents go to great lengths to emphasize this point.

This is a parable that teaches believers to be ready for the Lord's return at any time because we do not know when he will return. Readiness, however, is not a life lived in a state of red alert but rather a life characterized by watchfulness.

---

[1]The Nestle-Aland Greek New Testament places paragraph markers at 24:42, 24:45, 25:1, and 25:13 that support reading the parable in the larger context (24:42-25:13).

[ii] Arland J. Hultgren, *the Parables of Jesus: A Commentary* (Grand Rapids: William B. Eerdmans Publishing, 2000), 170. Hultgren claimed the parable falls within the Eschatological Discourse that describes events at the end of the world (Matthew 24:1-25:46).

[iii] Osborne, *Matthew*, 918.

[iv] Ibid., 917.

[v] Turner, *Matthew*, 592.

[vi] Richard T. France, "On Being Ready" in *the Challenge of Jesus' Parables*: ed. Richard N. Longenecker, (Grand Rapids: William B. Eerdmans Publishing, 2000), 178.

[vii] Ibid., 179.

[viii] Hultgren, *the Parables*, 170.

[ix] Snodgrass, *Stories*, 505.

[x] Hultgren, *the Parables*, 170.

[xi] Ibid.

[xii] Osborne, *Matthew*, 912.

[xiii] Ibid.

[xiv] Blomberg, *Interpreting*, 195.

[xv] Mounce, *Basics*, 245.

[xvi] Burge, Cohick, Green, *Antiquity*, 150.

[xvii] Osborne, *Matthew*, 916.

[xviii] Ibid.

[xix] Ibid.

[xx] France, "*On Being Ready*", 182.

[xxi] The quote is from the NIV translation.

[xxii] I am referring to my major professor in doctoral studies, Bill Warren.

[xxiii] Jonathan M. Butler and Ronald L. Numbers, Introduction in *The Disappointed: Millerism and Millenarianism in the Nineteenth Century* ed. by Ronald L. Numbers and Jonathan M. Butler (Knoxville: University of Tennessee Press, 1993), xv – xxi.

[xxiv] Stephen D. O'Leary, *Arguing the Apocalypse: A Theory of Millennial Rhetoric* (Oxford: Oxford University Press, 1994), 99.

[xxv]Ibid. 108.

[xxvi]Ibid.

[xxvii]Quoted in J. F. Maclear, "The Republic and the Millennium," in *The Religion of the Republic*, ed. Elwyn A. Smith, 191.

Chapter 10

Matthew 25:14 - 30 Commentary and Interpretation

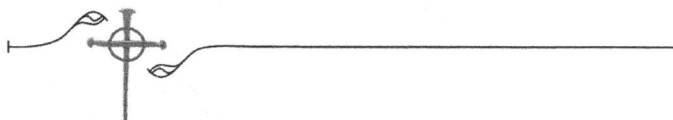

Great sermons teach believers there is far more to Christianity than just making a profession of faith. What are Christians called to do while we wait upon the Lord's return? Are we called to just sit and wait? Or is there something we should be doing? Matthew's parable of the talents answers these questions.

Like the parable of the ten virgins before it, Matthew's parable of the talents is a parable about readiness. This parable adds the element of working for the kingdom as a part of readiness,[i] but Matthew emphasizes the totality of the believer's efforts by using enormous sums of money.[ii] The parable sets the responsibility of the servants in terms of money, but the symbolism points to something more comprehensive.[iii] Craig Blomberg agreed; he claimed the parable reflects faithfulness to Jesus that leads to good stewardship of one's opportunities and abilities.[iv] Likewise, David Turner claimed the parable emphasized stewardship and structured the parable in the following format:

> **Distribution of Resources (25:15)**
> Five talents entrusted (25:15)
> Two talents entrusted (25:15)
> One talent entrusted (25:15)
> **Stewardship of Resources (25:16-18)**
> Five talents invested and five more earned (25:16)
> Two talents invested and two more earned (25:17)
> One talent hidden and nothing earned (25:18)

David W. Brown

> Reward for Stewardship (25:19-30)
> Good and Faithful slave rewarded (25:20-21)
> Good and Faithful slave rewarded (25:22-23)
> Wicked and lazy slave punished (25:24-30)[v]

The point here is that Matthew is placing an emphasis on stewardship, and believers are called to do far more than simply wait for Jesus' to return.

Before an exegesis of the parable is performed, a historical understanding of the setting is crucial, since the story begins on the footsteps of the temple (Matt. 24:1). Louis Feldman claimed the temple was loaded with an enormous amount of money. In a 2001 article, Feldman wrote that a Latin inscription on a stone plaque in Rome commemorating the coliseum verified this claim. The plaque revealed that the money taken out of the Jerusalem temple in A.D. 70 following its destruction paid for the construction of the Roman Coliseum.[vi] Archaeological evidence also exists supporting this claim as well. For example, Titus' arch features images of the Romans carrying away the treasures from the Jewish temple.

In the biblical world, one talent was equivalent to six thousand *denarii*, with one *denaraii* equating to a days wages.[vii] So the slave who was given five talents was handling more money than he could have expected in a lifetime.[viii] Since the vast majority of people in the Biblical world were poor, stockpiling enormous sums of money in the temple by the rich served only to highlight the economic dilemma that Matthew was making in the parable. In addition to stockpiling money in the temple, taxes levied on subject people were especially severe, as Luke Timothy Johnston claimed.[ix] He reported that under Julius Caesar, a quarter of a year's harvest could be taxed.[x] The compounding effect of stockpiling money in the temple by the religious elite, combined with local chieftains who were skimming even more from the people, served to heighten the bitterness that existed between the rich and poor.

As a result, Matthew is equating the wicked servant in the parable to the Pharisees who, for all practical purposes, were burying their money in the temple rather than investing it in the community where it could help the poor. Matthew is teaching that part of readiness for the Lord's return applies to Christian stewardship. If believers are not practicing good stewardship, they are not ready for the Lord's return.

Although the parable consists of only a single paragraph, the larger context must include Matthew 24:1-25:46. Within the larger context,

Matthew notes a fivefold emphasis of no one knowing the day or hour of the return of the master:[xi]

- * But concerning that day and hour, no one knows, not the angels of Heaven, nor the Son, but only the Father (24:36).
- * Be on alert, because no one knows what day your Lord will come (24:42).
- * For this reason, you also must be ready because the Son of Man comes at an hour you do not think he will (24:44).
- * The master of the slave comes on a day when he does not expect and an hour which he does not know (24:50).
- * Therefore, be on alert, for you do not know that day nor the hour (25:13).

Taken as a whole, these verses have a compounding effect that emphasizes the need for readiness. This leads to the main point Matthew is making, and that is believers are to be ready for the return of our heavenly master by serving him with all of our worldly resources, symbolized in the parable by enormous sums of money.

The first sub-point is that God entrusts all people with a portion of his resources and expects them to act as good stewards.[xii] This sub-point is supported by verses fourteen and fifteen. All too often in evangelical life, salvation is treated as an accomplishment piled up in our past. As a result, Christians have come to believe they have no responsibility in Christian service to God. David Turner claimed the three servants stand for the church, which is portrayed as a mixed community.[xiii] Craig Blomberg, however, rightly argued that the first two slaves are dealt with identically, and repeated phrasing indicates these two characters only have one role to play between them:[xiv]

- * Master you have entrusted five talents to me. See, I have gained five more talents (25:20).
- * Master you have entrusted two talents to me. See, I have gained two more talents (25:22).
- * His master said to him, "Well done, good and faithful slave. You were faithful in a few things, I will put you in charge of many things; enter into the joy of your master" (25:21).

> * His master said to him, "Well done, good and faithful slave. You were faithful in a few things, I will put you in charge of many things; enter into the joy of your master" (25:23).

The adverb "immediately" (*eutheos*) reflects the urgency of the slave's responses.[xv] The exact amounts of money of the first two slaves are not relevant, nor are their amounts of return. As a result, the emphasis is on the characteristic of fidelity rather than numerical success.[xvi] F.D. Bruner claimed the varying amounts show that everyone in the Kingdom of Christ is not created equally.[xvii] Likewise, Blomberg argued a similar point that while different people perform at different levels, all are expected to do their best as stewards.[xviii]

The second sub-point is that God's people will be faithfully rewarded for their service and participation, and this is supported by verses nineteen through twenty-three. The long delay highlights the master's return. Each of the first two slaves is described as "good and faithful," which refers to their participation and activity during the master's absence. The master rewards the two slaves heartily by assigning them much more responsibility in the kingdom. Entrance into the master's joy is most likely thought of as entrance into the eschatological feast or the great banquet that inaugurates the reign of Jesus upon his return.[xix] The point Matthew is making is they both invested, both received a return, and for that, they are both rewarded.[xx]

The third sub-point is that those who refuse to use God's gifts will be punished by separation from God, and this is supported by verses twenty-four through thirty.[xxi] Grant Osborne claimed the third servant was obviously fearful of the master and took the easy route by burying the money to keep it safe.[xxii] As a pastor, I find Osborne's comments right on target in church life. Over and over, I am given excuses by congregants that the reason they do not witness is because they do not feel they know enough about the Bible, and they do not want to lead anyone astray. A friend of mine once responded to this comment by claiming that people are destined for Hell without God, so in effect, the only change we can make upon their destiny is a positive one.

Nonetheless, these folks are similar to the third servant. They are fearful of their master and seek to take the easy way out by failing to participate. Ed Schweizer emphasized the same concept when he wrote,

"The message is not that God is a rapacious capitalist, but that he is not satisfied with inaction. To play it safe, to keep one's slate clean, is not good enough. God looks for more than a religion that is concerned with not doing anything wrong."[xxiii] Initially, the third servant appeared to be wise by taking no risk, but as Blomberg noted, "To make no commitment on religious matters is really to make a damning commitment by default."[xxiv] Good stewardship and participation during our master's absence determines whether or not we will enter into our master's joy.

David W. Brown

Money, Stewardship and the Second Coming of Christ:
Evaluating our Readiness in Light of the Coming of our Lord
Matthew 25:14-30

INTRODUCTION:
Theological Thrust:
> This is a parable about readiness, but Matthew adds the element of working for the kingdom as a part of readiness.

Structure:
> **Distribution of resources (25:15)**
>> Five talents entrusted (25:15)
>>> Two talents entrusted (25:15)
>>>> One talent entrusted (25:15)
>
> **Stewardship of Resources (25:16-18)**
>> Five talents invested and five more earned (25:16)
>>> Two talents invested and two more earned (25:17)
>>>> One talent hidden and nothing earned (25:18)
>
> **Reward for Stewardship (25:19-30)**
>> Good and Faithful slave rewarded (25:20-21)
>>> Good and Faithful slave rewarded (25:22-23)
>>>> Wicked and lazy slave punished (25:24-30)

Organization Emphasis:
> Although the parable consists of only a single paragraph, the larger context must include Matthew 24:1-25:46. Within the larger context, Matthew notes a fivefold emphasis of no one knowing the day or hour of the return of the master. The fivefold emphasis heightens the idea of readiness.
>> * But concerning that day and hour no one knows, not the angel of Heaven, nor the Son, but only the Father (Matt. 24:36).
>> * Be on alert, because no one knows what day your Lord will come (Matt. 24:42).
>> * For this reason, you also must be ready, because the Son of Man comes at an hour you do not think he will (Matt. 24:44).
>> * The master of the slave comes on a day when he does not expect and an hour which he does not know (Matt. 24:50).

> * Therefore, be on alert, for you do not know that day nor the hour (Matt. 25:13).

Setting:
> Matthew is equating the wicked servant in the parable to the Pharisees who, for all practical purposes, were burying their money in the temple rather than investing it in the community where it could help the poor.

Main Point:
> Believers are to be ready for the return of our heavenly master by serving him with all of our worldly resources, symbolized in the parable by enormous sums of money.

BODY:
Sub-Points:
> **I. God entrusts all people with a portion of his resources and expects them to act as good stewards (25:14-15).**
>> A) Turner claimed the three servants stand for the church, which is portrayed as a mixed community.
>> B) Oftentimes in evangelical life, salvation is treated as an accomplishment piled up in our past.
>>> i. As a result, believers come to believe they have no responsibility in Christian service to God.
>>> ii. Believers are called to serve God with all of the talents he has endowed us with.
>
> **II. God's people will be faithfully rewarded for their service and participation (25:19-23).**
>> A) Each of the first two slaves is described as "good and faithful," which refers to their participation and activity during the master's absence.
>>> i. The master rewards the two slaves heartily by assigning them much more responsibility in the kingdom.
>>> ii. Entrance into the master's joy is entrance into the eschatological feast or the great banquet that inaugurates the reign of Jesus upon his return.
>>> iii. The point Matthew is making is they both invested, both received a return, and for that, they are both rewarded.

III. Those who refuse to use God's gifts will be punished by separation from God (25:24-30).
    A) Grant Osborne claimed the third servant was obviously fearful of the master and took the easy route by burying the money to keep it safe.
        i. As a pastor, I find Osborne's comments right on target in church life. Over and over again, I am given excuses by congregants that the reason they do not witness is because they do not feel they know enough about the Bible, and they don't want to lead anyone astray.
        ii. A friend of mine once responded to this comment by claiming that people are destined for Hell without God, so in effect. The only change we can make upon their destiny is a positive one.
    B) Some believers are similar to the third servant. They are fearful of their master and seek to take the easy way out by failing to participate.
        i. Blomberg noted, "To make no commitment on religious matters is really to make a damning commitment by default."
    C) Good stewardship and participation during our master's absence determines whether or not we will enter into our master's joy.

SUMMATION:

This is a parable that teaches about readiness. Part of our readiness is defined by working for the Kingdom of God. Matthew emphasizes the totality of the believer's efforts by using enormous sums of money. God entrusts all people with a portion of his resources, and he expects his servants to participate in his redemptive plan. One day, God will return, and he will reward those who have shown fidelity to him and punish those who have not.

Final Thoughts:

Christianity is not a religion that tolerates laziness. Some evangelicals over-emphasize the concept of grace as a means to justify their lack of participation in service. However, God expects his servants to be working until his return. Christians are called to do more than play it safe and to keep our slates clean. God will heartily reward those who have invested their efforts into the community of God, as well as punish those who have not. The pastor/teacher must grasp that Matthew is using enormous sums of money to describe the totality of the servants' efforts. This parable teaches believers that we are to be prepared for our Lord's return, whenever that may be.

---

[i] Osborne, *Matthew*, 920.

[ii] Ibid.

[iii] Donald A. Hagner, Word Biblical Commentary (Dallas, Word Book Publishing, 1995), 733.

[iv] Craig Blomberg, *The New American Commentary: Matthew* (Nashville: Broadman Press, 1992), 371-2.

[v] Turner, *Matthew*, 599.

[vi] Louis H Feldman, "Financing the Colosseum" in *Biblical Archaeology Review*; Jul/Aug 2001; 27, 4. Feldman claimed the transcription read: "The Emperor Titus Caesar Vespasian Augustus ordered the new amphitheater to be made from the (proceeds from the sale of the) booty."

[vii] Marvin A. Powell, "Weights and Measures," in *The Anchor Bible Dictionary*: vol. 6 (ed. David Noel Freedman: New York: Doubleday Publishing, 1992), 907-8.

[viii] Osborne, *Matthew*, 920.

[ix] Luke Timothy Johnston, *The Writings of the New Testament*, Third Edition (Minneapolis: Fortress Press, 2010), 24.

[x] Ibid.

[xi] Snodgrass, *Stories*, 526.

[xii] Blomberg, *Interpreting*, 214.

[xiii] Turner, *Matthew*, 598.

[xiv] Ibid.

[xv] Turner, *Matthew*, 601.

[xvi] Ibid.

[xvii] F.D. Bruner, *The Christbook*, (Waco: Word Publishing, 1987), 100.

[xviii] Blomberg, *Matthew*, 372.

[xix] Turner, *Matthew*, 601.

[xx] Blomberg, *Interpreting*, 214.

[xxi] Ibid.

[xxii] Osborne, *Matthew*, 926.

[xxiii] Eduard Schweizer, *The Good News According to Matthew*, trans. D. E. Green, (Atlanta: John Knox Publishing, 1975), 473.

[xxiv] Blomberg, *Matthew*, 372.

Sermons about Character Formation

David W. Brown

Chapter 11

Matthew 7:13 - 29
Commentary and Interpretation

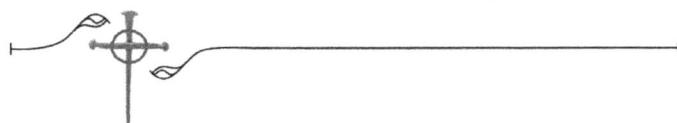

Great sermons do far more than entertain. They are designed to instruct believers then move them from knowing and understanding the Scriptures to living out those understandings as they go through life. Great sermons inform the choices we make in life, and from this perspective, they shape the character of believers. When sermons fail to educate and inform believers on the importance of Christian doctrines, we begin to view Scripture as having little significance to our lives. The failure to educate Christians on doctrinal beliefs of the Bible is crucial for the Christian believer because Scripture that is viewed as having little importance upon the life of the believer does not impress upon him/her the need to serve and participate in God's redemptive plan. Over time, the believer begins to see his/her role as that of a spectator in the Christian faith and eventually falls away. This passage places the importance of character formation center stage.

The overall context of Matthew's Sermon on the Mount sets the tone for character formation of the believer, since Matthew has been building to a climax from chapter five. According to Grant Osborne, the context of this exposition has involved the believer's relationship to Jesus and the new community (5:17- 48) and the priority of God in every aspect of our religious life (6:19-34), as well as our relations to material possessions (7:1-12).[i] Now, the time has come to make a choice, and the believer must recognize the serious nature of this choice.[ii]

Although the passage contains multiple paragraphs, from a literary perspective, it breaks down into three metaphorical pairs of two gates, two trees, and two houses. David Turner breaks the passage down as follows:

* Two gates/ways (7:13-14)
* Two trees/fruits (7:15-23)
* Two houses/foundations (7:24-27)

However, the passage does more than simply break down into three pairs. Each of these metaphorical pairs is a catalyst to the character formation of the believer.[iv] The application of these metaphors is listed below:

* Two gates that open to two different destinations, each of which shape the character of the individual
* Two trees that bear two different fruits, each of which shapes the character of the individual
* Two houses that describe two different foundations, each of which shape the character of the individual

From the paths we take to the fruit we bear, and also to the foundations of our faith, each of these specific areas shapes the character of who we are as Christian believers. This leads to the main point of the passage: Matthew is attempting to move the believer from simply listening to God's word to acting upon it, which will allow God to mold and shape our character as believers and move us from who we are today into what he desires for us be tomorrow.

The first sub-point is that character formation is determined by the paths we take in life, and this is supported by verses thirteen and fourteen. The first pair of metaphors describes two gates that open to two distinct ways. The choice of which path to take is a crucial one, and this question has been posed to every generation for centuries. Craig Blomberg noted that the genre of two ways was well-known in Jewish literature.[v] Jewish literature not only emphasized the narrow way, but also that those on the narrow path bore good fruit. Likewise, David Turner summarized the choice of the two paths this way: "Those who take the easy road find to their horror that it leads to the most difficult destination imaginable. But those who take the difficult path of the kingdom arrive joyously in the kingdom to experience life with the Father."[vi]

In addition, while the gates open to two ways, Matthew commands (*eiselthate*) the believer to enter.[vii] Osborne claimed this command was a powerful warning against taking the easy path in life. "The Christian life was never meant to be easy, and true followers are expected to work hard at aligning their lives with these exhortations."[viii] Also, the verb *eiselthate* is used in an active voice. In the Greek active voice, the subject, which is a plural you, initiates the action.[ix] In other words, believers cannot ride a fence on the issue of which path to take in life, and Matthew is attempting to force the believer into making a decision. The choice is critical, since it connects our destiny with eschatological judgment.[x] The emphasis is that the path that we take in life shapes our Christian character. The narrow path is one that requires sacrifice and suffering, but the end result is a path that brings eternal peace.

The second sub-point is that character formation requires that we develop spiritual discernment, and this is supported by verses fifteen through twenty. Verse fifteen opens with another Greek imperative verb. This one (*prosechete*) is typically translated as "beware" or "watch out."[xi] Believers are to watch out for false shepherds who will steal the sheep and then abandon them when Satan/the wolf comes.[xii] In Ephesians 4:14, Paul wrote to the church of Ephesus specifically addressing the problem of wolves that devour the flock. Blaine Charette claimed the identity of the false prophets is kept deliberately vague, so that verses fifteen through twenty-three can have a "wide and continuing application."[xiii] As a result, the present tense of the verb (*prosechete*) calls for constant vigilance.[xiv] All of these grammatical issues indicate the need for spiritual insight; believers must have this characteristic in order to recognize false prophets when they appear.

In the next paragraph, Matthew uses the metaphor of fruit to refer to the totality of one's deeds in life. This would include everything from what we say to how we live. The metaphor was quite common in the ancient world. The Greek philosopher Philo compared young people to plants that were cultivated and grown until they bore the fruit of goodness on their stem.[xv] Paul also wrote to the Colossian believers using the same metaphorical analogy of bearing fruit and good deeds.[xvi] Likewise, Matthew uses the same familiar analogy. In addition, verses sixteen through twenty form an *inclusio* that frames the section and describes what type of fruit the believer is to beware of in life. The structure can be seen below:

> * **You will know them by their fruits (7:16a)**
> - Grapes and figs (*good fruit*) are not gathered from bad trees (7:16b)
> - Good trees bear good fruit; bad trees bear bad fruit (7:17)
> - Good trees cannot produce bad fruit, nor bad trees good fruit (7:18)
> - Trees that do not bear good fruit (Christian discipleship) will be cut down (7:19)
>
> * **You will know them by their fruits (7:20)**

The problem of false teachers was regularly recorded in the New Testament and continues to persist even today. Pastors/teachers must be on guard regularly against false teaching in our sermons and teaching outlines. The point of this section is that the saints must have a spirit of discernment and be on a constant lookout for people who can lead them astray in their faith. The purpose of constant vigilance is to consider the fruits of every person and separate the good from the bad and the wolves from the shepherds.[xvii]

The third sub-point is that the foundations that we lay form the character of the believer, and this concept is supported by verses twenty-four through twenty-seven. In these verses, Jesus teaches that a person stands or falls based upon his/her relation to God's words.[xviii] The story of the two builders is designed primarily to contrast those who simply hear with those who actually go and build their faith. Matthew used two present tense verbs to connect the relationship between hearing and doing. By making this connection, Jesus enables believers to visualize the true standard by which decisions are made and character is shaped.[xix] The on-going type of action described in verse twenty-four is compared to a wise man who heeds the advice then goes and builds his house on rock.

In addition, Matthew described a storm with a destructive force from multiple angles. The battering winds with heavy rains and floods that follow depict the harrowing nature of the storm. Grant Osborne noted the word play in verse twenty-five between the words "beat against" (*prosepesan*) and "fall" (*epesen*) emphasizes the durability of a house built wisely.[xx] By contrast, a fool does not heed the words of wisdom but builds his house on sand. The notion of a fool rejecting wisdom is not unique to the New Testament, and both the Psalms and Proverbs depict the fool as one who leaves God out of his/her life.[xxi] In this case, the torrential wind, rain, and floods were too much for the house to stand. Verse twenty-seven denotes a literary progression that is held together by the conjunction "and," which is repeated five times in rapid-fire succession:

- * and the rain fell,
- * and the river came,
- * and the wind blew,
- * and struck against the house,
- * and great was its fall.

The point Matthew is emphasizing is the house did not simply fall; it fell because the builder regularly failed to heed the wisdom of Jesus' words, and this continual failure influenced the character of who he was.

David W. Brown

Two Gates, Two Trees, and Two Houses:
Pairing up to Make a Point about Character Formation
Matthew 7:13-29

INTRODUCTION:

Larger Context:

The larger context of the Sermon on the Mount has involved:
* The believer's relationship to Jesus and the new community (5:17-48)
* The priority of God in every aspect of our religious life (6:19-34)
* Our relations to material possessions (7:1-12)

Now, the time has come to make a choice, and the believer must recognize the serious nature of this choice.

Choices as Metaphors:

Each of these metaphorical pairs is a catalyst to the character formation of the believer:
* Two gates that open to two different destinations, each of which shape the character of the believer (7:13-14).
* Two trees that bear two different fruits, each of which shapes the character of the believer (7:15-23).
* Two houses that describe two different foundations, each of which shape the character of the believer (7:24-27).

Main Point:

Matthew is attempting to move the believer from simply listening to God's word to acting upon it, so that He can mold and shape the character of the believer from who we are today into who God desires for us to be tomorrow.

BODY:

Sub-Points:

I. Character formation is determined by the path we choose to take in life (7:13-14).

  A) The choice of which path to take is a crucial one, and this question has been posed to every generation for centuries. Craig Blomberg noted that the genre of two ways was well known in Jewish literature (Our generation is not unique).

      i. Although the gates open to two ways, Matthew commands (*eiselthate*) the believer to enter.
      ii. Osborne claimed this command was a powerful warning against taking the easy path in life. "The Christian life was never meant to be easy, and true followers are expected to work hard at aligning their lives with these exhortations."
      iii. The verb "to enter" (*eiselthate*) is used in an active voice.
      iv. In the Greek active voice, the subject, which is a plural you, initiates the action. Believers cannot ride a fence on the issue of which path to take in life, and Matthew is attempting to force the believer into making a decision.

II. **Character formation requires that we develop spiritual discernment (7:15-20).**
    A) The verb (*prosechete*) is typically translated as "beware" or "watch out."
      i. Believers are to "watch out" for false shepherds who will steal the sheep then abandon them when Satan/the wolf comes.
      ii. Matthew uses the metaphor of fruit to refer to the totality of one's deeds in life. This would include everything from what we say to how we live.
      iii. The metaphor was quite common in the ancient world.
      Three examples:
        1. The Greek philosopher Philo compared young people to plants that were cultivated and grown until they bore the fruit of goodness on their stem.
        2. Paul also wrote to the Colossian believers using the same metaphorical analogy of bearing fruit and good deeds.
        3. Matthew's analogy.
    B) You will know them by their fruits (7:16).
      i. Grapes and figs (*good fruit*) are not gathered from bad trees (7:16b)
      ii. Good trees bear good fruit; bad trees bear bad fruit (7:17).
      iii. Good trees cannot produce bad fruit, nor bad trees good fruit (7:18).
      iv. Trees that do not bear good fruit (Christian discipleship) will be cut down (7:19).
    C) You will know them by their fruits (7:20).

i. The point of this section is that the saints must have a spirit of discernment and be on a constant lookout for people who can lead them astray in their faith.
   ii. The purpose of constant vigilance is to consider the fruits of every Christian and separate the good from the bad and the wolves from the shepherds.
III. **The foundations we lay form the character the believer (7:14-27).**
   A) Jesus teaches that a person stands or falls based upon his/her relation to his words.
      i. The story of the two builders contrasts those who simply hear with those who actually go and build their faith.
   B) Matthew used two present tense verbs to connect the relationship between hearing and doing.
      i. By making this connection, Jesus enables believers to visualize the true standard by which decisions are made and character is shaped.
      ii. The word play in verse twenty-five between the words "beat against" (*prosepesan*) and "fall" (*epesen*) emphasizes the durability of a house built wisely.
   C) Verse twenty-seven denotes a literary progression that is connected by the conjunction "and," which is repeated five times in rapid-fire succession:
      * and the rain fell,
      * and the river came,
      * and the wind blew,
      * and struck against the house,
      * and great was its fall.
      i. Matthew is emphasizing that the house did not simply fall; it fell because the builder regularly failed to heeds wisdom of Jesus' words.

SUMMATION:

The choices we make in life impact and shape the character of who we are as believers, and these choices in life are described metaphorically in pairs of three. The first pairs are two gates that open to two different destinations, each of which shape the character of the believer. The second are two trees that bear two different fruits, each of which shapes the character of the believer. The third pairs are two houses that describe two different foundations, each of which shape the character of the believer. God's wisdom shapes the character of who we are by forcing the believer to recognize the serious nature of the choices we make in life.

Final Thoughts:

This passage places the importance of character formation center stage. It is a passage that teaches believers that the choices we make in life form the character of who we are today and our destinies, who we will be tomorrow. Matthew is emphasizing that the time has come to make a choice, and the believer must recognize the serious nature of this choice.

---

[i] Osborne, *Matthew*, 266.

[ii] Ibid.

[iii] Turner, *Matthew*, 214.

[iv] Charles H. Talbert, *Reading the Sermon on the Mount: Character Formation and Decision Making in Matthew 5-7* (Columbia: University of South Carolina Press, 2004), 138-46.

[v] Blomberg, *Matthew*, 713. Deut. 30:15-20; 2 Esdr 7:1-16; *Did.* 1:1-6:7.

[vi] Turner, *Matthew*, 216.

[vii] Mounce, *Basics*, 312. The verb *eiselthate* is an aorist active imperative.

[viii] Osborne, *Matthew*, 269.

[ix] Daniel B. Wallace, *Greek Grammar: Beyond the Basics* (Grand Rapids: Zondervan Publishing, 1996), 410.

[x] Turner, *Matthew*, 214.

[xi] The NASB translates the verb *prosechete* as "Beware" while the NIV translates the verb as "Watch out."

[xii] Osborne, *Matthew*, 278.

[xiii] Blaine Charette, The Theme of Recompense in Matthew's Gospel in the Journal for the *Study of the New Testament* Supplement Series 79, Sheffield Press, December 1992, 125.

[xiv] Mounce, *Basics*, 315. Present tense verbs denote a continuous type of action.

[xv] C. D. Young, *The Works of Philo: New Updated Version* (Peabody: Hendrickson Publishing, 2008), 623.

[xvi] Colossians 1:10 encourages the Colossian believers to walk worthy of the Lord and to please Him in all respects, bearing fruit in all good works, and growing in the knowledge of God.

[xvii] Osborne, *Matthew*, 273.

[xviii] Talbert, *Reading*, 143.

[xix] Talbert, *Reading*, 143.

[xx] Osborne, *Matthew*, 276.

[xxi] See Psalm 14:1; 53:1 and Proverbs 12:15-16; 14:33.

Chapter 12

Ecclesiastes 1:1 - 11
Commentary and Interpretation

Great sermons teach believers about character formation and priorities in life. More specifically, great sermons teach that true wisdom and happiness do not come through learning to balance the various aspects of our lives, but through learning to prioritize life with God as the top priority. The book of Ecclesiastes teaches this theme.

In order to grasp the setting of Ecclesiastes, one must first discern who wrote the book and what time period the book dates to. This is easier said than done, since theological debate rages over the dating and authorship of the book.[i] Tremper Longman and Raymond Dillard refer to the view that dates Ecclesiastes to the tenth century B.C. and Solomon as the author, as the "traditional" view.[ii] The term *Qohelet*, often spoken of in the book, literally means "assembler."[iii] The "traditional" view associates Solomon as the assembler because the root of this name "assemble" appears frequently in 1 Kings 8, when Solomon assembled the people at the dedication to the temple.[iv] Also, the *Qohelet* identifies himself as a King and a son of David in Ecclesiastes 1:1-2. These explicit statements, connected with Solomon's well-established reputation as a teacher of wisdom, confirm Solomonic authorship and date in the minds of many.[v]

The "critical" view of date and authorship, however, has good points as well. For example, if Solomon was the author of Ecclesiastes, why use the pseudonym *Qohelet*? What need would there be for Solomon to hide his identity?[vi] This view dates the book to the late postexilic period but prior to the Maccabean revolt.[vii] In addition, proponents of this view claim the syntax of the Hebrew and Aramaic push the book to a late date.[viii] However, D. C. Fredericks' thorough investigation into the linguistic arguments used to support a late date claimed these arguments were unpersuasive.[ix] In addition, Longman added that so little is known about the transmission of the biblical text during its earliest stages that we cannot rule out linguistic updating.[x] Thus, the so-called late forms may reflect updates on vocabulary and grammar by later scribes so their contemporaries could understand the book better.[xi]

Longman and Dillard claimed that as far as the book of Kings is concerned, Solomon never returned to a strong devotion to the Lord, and the split between the northern and southern kingdoms in 1 Kings 12 is attributed to his sin.[xii] This is enormously important not only from an interpretational perspective, but also from the perspective of character formation. The fact that such profound and godly wisdom came from a man who eventually turned away from the Lord was too much for some, so an early tradition emerged that an older, repentant Solomon wrote the book to show the evils of his apostasy to the young.[xiii] Thus, the setting of an old, wise, repentant king emerged for Ecclesiastes. Longman, however, advocates that an editorial seam exists at 1:1-11 and 12:8-14, as this final editor (a second unnamed wisdom teacher) to the book reflects back onto the past life and work of the *Qohelet*.[xiv] Proponents claim this setting combined with the instructional section of the book supports Solomonic authorship.

The literary devices in Ecclesiastes are quite profound and easy to spot, and one of the first deals with superscriptions. A superscription is an introductory verse or verses at the beginning of a book that describe the content of the book, and they appear on several occasions throughout the various books of the Bible. According to Longman, the first eleven verses of Ecclesiastes is a superscription, but some scholars claim the superscription in Ecclesiastes is smaller.[xv]

All of this historical and literary evidence suggests that Solomon was the not only the *Qohelet*, but a man who, in the process of turning away from God, would attempt to fill this spiritual vacancy with material objects. This leads to the main point of the passage, and that is apart from God, people gain nothing from all of their toil.[xvi]

The first sub-point is life without God is nothing but futility, and this is supported by verse two. The vanity of vanities phrase in 1:2 and 12:8

forms an *inclusio* over the entire book. When applied to Solomon's life, the phrase produces an image of emptiness. Even with all he accomplished, Solomon's life had amounted to nothing from a spiritual perspective.

In his book, *Can Man Live Without God*, Ravi Zacharias described this same type of contrast in his depiction of the movie *Chariots of Fire*. The movie chronicled the lives of two Olympic runners: Harold Abrams and Eric Little. Each ran with equal passion, but their goals were completely opposite. Abrams ran for personal glory and personal recognition while Little ran out of Christian commitment for the sake of God.[xvii] As each runner prepared, competed, and won his respective race, Zacharias eloquently recorded the results. He wrote:

> And so it was that Abrams walked away amid thundering applause after winning the gold medal in the one hundred meters-but with a silence of despondency within. The downward tug is already underway. By contrast, Eric Little ran the four hundred meters and won. But more than that, he packed his bags and went on to China as a missionary to a cause greater than himself-the gold medal was put in its place, and his heart was completely at peace. [xviii]

Zacharias' point was that "the world of personal glory moves from triumph to emptiness because it can never deliver the fulfillment of the spirit of God."[xix] Despite all of the accomplishments Solomon could claim he had achieved in life, the same spiritual void left his heart empty because personal triumphs will never be able to fill the spiritual void that exists in the human heart.

The second sub-point is that most people will not make sense of this futility. This sub-point is supported by verses three through eight. In addition to the book being framed by the phrase "vanity of vanities," which appears in 1:2 and in 12:8 and forms an *inclusio* for the entire book,[xx] the phrase summarizes the thoughts of the *Qohelet* and his attitude toward life. The author's thoughts about the futility of life are best viewed in a series of repetitive cycles that appear in the text the *Qohelet* is unable to control. These cycles are listed below:

* Generations that come and go (1:4)
* A sun that rises and sets (1:5)
* A wind that goes round and round (1:6)
* Rivers that flow into the sea, but the sea does not fill up (1:7)[xxi]

All of these repetitive patterns continue regardless of man's efforts. These cycles serve to illustrate the idea of repetition in life that the *Qohelet* has no control over, and this constant repetition serves as a catalyst that adds to his sense of frustration. In verse three, the author cites another aspect of frustration: people gain nothing from their toil. Likewise, Sidney Greidinaus pointed out a similar pattern of antithetical parallelism that exists in verse eight that expresses the futility and frustration of the *Qohelet's* life:

* A *man*   is not able   to *speak*.
* An *eye*   is not satisfied   with *seeing*.
* An *ear*   is not filled   with *hearing*.[xxii]

Once again, this verse serves to underline the *Qohelet's* thoughts of futility and that life amounts to a chasing after the wind. In his mind, there is no reward for the toil of life, and the description by the *Qohelet* leaves nothing out.[xxiii] The pattern in verse eight is designed to capture the totality of the human senses (hearing, speaking, seeing), and all of these senses serve only to undermine his frustration.[xxiv]

The last sub-point is that true change comes from heaven and not earth, and this is supported by verse nine. The *Qohelet* stated in verses three and nine, "There is nothing new under the sun." This point is emphasized through repetition, since repeated words and phrases place an emphasis on the context they are embedded in. One of the struggles befallen by the *Qohelet* is that he spent an inordinate amount of time focused on material gain. Chapter two frames the author's worldview in the context of this self-centered and materialistic pattern:

* I built houses for myself (2:4)
* I made gardens and parks for myself (2:5)
* I made ponds of water for myself (2:6)
* I bought male and female slaves (2:7)
* I collected for myself silver and gold (2:8)

The point here is that if these endless cycles of futility are ever going to come to an end in our lives, believers must look for the change to come from God in Heaven rather than a world centered on itself. The *Qohelet* felt as though his life mimicked the same patterns of endless repetition of which he had no control over; generations that had come and gone, a sun that rose and set without meaning, wind that went round and round with no end. To him, life was meaningless because he was attempting to fill a spiritual void with worldly, material gain. This is so important for character formation in the life of the believer because true change that brings calm to a restless heart and peace to our chaotic lives can only come from God. The *Qohelet* is making the point that our focus should be on change that comes from Heaven rather than earth.

David W. Brown

The Futility of Mankind's Endeavors without God:
Life without God amounts to Nothing
Ecclesiastes 1:1-11

INTRODUCTION:
Authorship & Date:
The "traditional" view associates Solomon as the *Qohelet* or the assembler because the root of this name "assemble" appears frequently in 1 Kings 8 when Solomon assembled the people at the dedication to the temple. The "critical" view dates the book to the late postexilic period but prior to the Maccabean revolt. Proponents of this view claim the syntax of the Hebrew and Aramaic pushes the book to a late date.

Literary Devices:
* The phrase "vanity of vanities" is mentioned in both 1:2 and 12:8 and frames the entire book.
* The first eleven verses of Ecclesiastes is a superscription.
* An editorial seam exists at 1:1-11 and 12:8-14, as this final editor (a second unnamed wisdom teacher) to the book reflects back onto the past life and work of the *Qohelet*.

Main Point:
The main point of the passage is that apart from God, people gain nothing from all of their toil.

BODY:
Sub-Points:
I. Life without God is nothing but futility (1:2).
A) The phrase "vanity of vanities" in 1:2 and 12:8 forms an *inclusio* around the entire book.
  i. When applied to the life of Solomon, the phrase reflects an image of emptiness.
  ii. The image of emptiness, when applied to Solomon's life, provides a contrast.
    - The contrast: How could someone who had accomplished so much feel so empty?

B) In his book, *Can Man Live Without God*, Ravi Zacharias described this same type of contrast in his depiction of the movie *Chariots of Fire*.
  i. The movie chronicled the lives of two Olympic runners, Harold Abrams and Eric Little.
  ii. Each ran with equal passion, but their goals were completely opposite.
  iii. Abrams ran for personal glory and personal recognition, while Little ran out of Christian commitment to God.
  iv. Zacharias' point was that "the world of personal glory moves from triumph to emptiness because it can never deliver the fulfillment of the spirit of God."

II. **Most people will not make sense of this futility (1:3-8).**
  A) The author's thoughts about the futility of life are best viewed in a series of repetitive cycles that appear in the text the *Qohelet* is unable to control.
   * Generations that come and go (1:4)
   * A sun that rises and sets (1:5)
   * A wind that goes round and round (1:6)
   * Rivers that flow into the sea, but the sea does not fill up (1:7)
  B) These cycles serve to illustrate the idea of repetition in life that the *Qohelet* has no control over, and this constant repetition serves as a catalyst that adds to his sense of frustration.
   i. A similar pattern of antithetical parallelism exists in verse eight that expresses the futility of life:
   - A *man*   is not able   to *speak*.
   - An *eye*   is not satisfied   with *seeing*.
   - An *ear*   is not filled   with *hearing*.
   ii. The same pattern is emphasized once again; this verse serves to underline the *Qohelet*'s thoughts of futility and that life amounts to a chasing after the wind.

III. **True change comes from Heaven, not from earth (1:9).**
  A) The *Qohelet* stated in verses three and nine, "There is nothing new under the sun."
   i. This point is emphasized through repetition, since repeated words and phrases place an emphasis.

B) The *Qohelet* spent an inordinate amount of time focused on material gain.
  i. Chapter two frames the author's worldview in the context of this self-centered and materialistic pattern:
     - I built houses for myself (2:4)
     - I made gardens and parks for myself (2:5)
     - I made ponds of water for myself (2:6)
     - I bought male and female slaves (2:7)
     - I collected for myself silver and gold (2:8)
  ii. The point here is that if these endless cycles of futility are ever going to come to an end, the change must come from God in Heaven rather than from a world of people centered around ourselves.
  iii. The *Qohelet* felt as though his life mimicked the same patterns of endless repetition, which he had no control over, generations that had come and gone, a sun that rose and set without meaning, wind that went round and round with no end.
  iv. To him, life was meaningless because he was attempting to fill a spiritual void with worldly, material gain.
  v. True change that calms the heart and brings peace to our chaotic lives can only come from God.

SUMMATION:
This is a passage that teaches about character formation and that true wisdom and happiness do not come through learning to balance the various aspects of our lives, but by learning to prioritize life with God as the top priority.

Final Thoughts:
To grasp the meaning of this passage, one must first recognize the literary devices that exist in the text. These repeated phrases encompass the meaning of this passage and the book as a whole. True change in life does not come from accumulating material possessions. True change only comes from God. Only He can bring a sense of peace to our chaotic lives.

[i] Duane A. Garret, *The New American Commentary: An Exegetical and Theological Exposition of Holy Scripture NIV Text*, Proverbs Ecclesiastes Song of Songs, vol. 14, (Nashville: Broadman Press, 1993), 254-67.

[ii] Tremper Longman III & Raymond B. Dilliard, *An Introduction to the Old Testament*, Second Edition, (Grand Rapids, Zondervan Publishing, 1994), 280.

[iii] Gary D. Pratico and Miles V. Van Pelt, *Basics of Biblical Hebrew Grammar*, Second Edition, (Grand Rapids, Zondervan Publishing, 2007), 285.

[iv] Longman & Dilliard, *Introduction*, 279. The root appears seven times in chapter eight alone.

[v] Ibid., See also Garret, *Ecclesiastes*, 282.

[vi] Ibid., 281.

[vii] Ibid.

[viii] Franz Delitzsch, *Proverbs, Ecclesiastes and Song of Solomon* (Grand Rapids: Eerdmans Publishing, 1975), 190.

[ix] D. C. Fredericks, "Qohelet's Language: Re-evaluating Its Nature and Date" in the *Ancient Near Eastern Texts*, 3rd edition, ed. J.B. Pritchard (New York: Edwin Melen Publishing, 1988), 301.

[x] Tremper Longman III, *The New International Commentary on the Old Testament*, The Book of Ecclesiastes (Grand Rapids: William B. Eerdmans Publishing 1998), 10.

[xi] Ibid.

[xii] Longman & Dillard, *Introduction*, 280.

[xiii] Ibid.

[xiv] Longman, *Ecclesiastes*, 57.

[xv] Sidney Greidanus, *Preaching Christ from Ecclesiastes: Foundations for Expository Sermons* (Grand Rapids: William B. Eerdmans Publishing, 2010), 34. Greidanaus claimed the superscription was regulated to verse one.

[xvi] Greidinaus, *Preaching*, 39.

[xvii] Ravi Zacharias, *Can Man Live Without God* (Nashville: W Publishing Group, 1994), 152.

[xviii] Ibid.

[xix] Ibid.

[xx] Greidinaus, *Preaching*, 31.

[xxi] Greidinaus, *Preaching*, 34.

[xxii] Ibid., 45.

[xxiii] Longman, *Ecclesiastes*, 65.

[xxiv] Greidinaus, *Preaching*, 45-48.

Chapter 13

James 3:1 - 12
Commentary and Interpretation

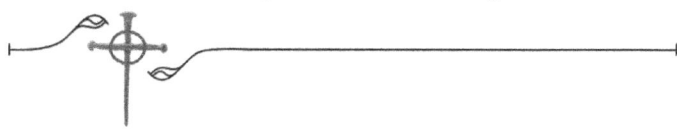

Great sermons do more than simply link together good works and righteous thought. Great sermons fuse together ethical behavior and the wisdom of God, so that the believer sees the two as forever intertwined. The epistle of James accomplishes this task. This passage combines the use of a number of metaphors to vividly describe the wisdom of God that shapes the character of the Christian believer.

Originally, the book was thought of as little more than a collection of ethical instructions for the Christian believer.[i] In fact, Martin Luther saw little value in the book and referred to it as an "Epistle of Straw."[ii] A study of some of the literary devices and their functions, however, reflects that James is much more complex than originally thought. This passage begins (3:1) and ends (3:12) with the phrase "my brothers" (*adelphoi mou*).[iii] By framing the passage this way, James not only develops an argument for mature speech and its relationship to his Christian brothers, but also identifies the starting and stopping points for the passage.[iv]

Also, this passage is followed by a section (3:13-18) dealing with wisdom, and this is not the first time James has paired speech and wisdom together. As Craig Blomberg and Mariam Kamell noted, James has made this connection before in chapter one.[v] By combining speech and wisdom, this literary unit serves to introduce the issue of quarrelling within the church in chapter four.[vi]

According to Kurt Richardson, the passage is broken down by a series of metaphorical analogies about the tongue:

1. The Responsibility of the Teacher (3:1)
2. The Uncontrollable Tongue (3:2-8)
   (1) Analogies of Size (3:2-5)
   (2) Analogies of Force (3:6-8)
   (3) Analogies of Incompatibility (3:9-12)[vii]

Richardson's concise organization of the passage views the tongue as a source of greatness.[viii] When controlled, the tongue can be used for the greatness of Christian teaching. However, when left unchecked, the tongue can be used for great evil, and these incompatibilities are a reflection of a Christian who has failed to mature. This leads to the main point of the passage: the tongue is presented as the key to self-control for a virtuous life.[ix] By bringing the tongue under control, the whole self can be guided into well-doing.[x]

The first sub-point is Christians should not aspire to become a teacher too hastily,[xi] and this is supported by verse one. The role of the teacher is one for the mature believer. Christian teachers depend heavily upon the tongue and will, therefore, be judged more strictly. The verb translated as "become" (*ginesthe*) is a present imperative. In Greek, the imperative mood is used when making a command.[xii] In addition, James separates the negative (not) from the verb (become) for emphasis.[xiii] Blomberg and Kamell pointed out that the negative imperative "not... should become" could imply to "stop becoming" and suggests that some in the congregation were using the position to attain status.[xiv] This, combined with the issue of quarrelling in the church that James addresses in chapter four, supports Blomberg's and Kamell's point. Teachers depend heavily upon the tongue and should take the role all the more seriously. The fact that teaching is almost exclusively an oral form of communication means that it is potentially dangerous and should be entered into with caution and reverence. Dan McCartney pointed out that teaching has the potential to not only destroy the teacher, but to harm the students.[xv]

The second sub-point is that Christians must learn to control the tongue, and this is supported by verses two through eight. There are a couple of literary devices that reflect that these verses should be interpreted together. First, the author uses a series of analogies that reflect both positive and negative uses of something small controlling something that is large:

> Positive examples
> * A small bit controlling a large horse (3:3)
> * A small rudder steering a large ship (3:4)
>
> Negative examples
> * A small tongue boasting of great/large accomplishments (3:5)
> * A small spark starting a large forest fire (3:6)

Second, the phrase "the whole body" (*holon to soma*) is used three times in this passage (3:2, 3, and 6) to describe both positive and negative uses of the tongue. Verses three and four give two positive examples of something small controlling something large, while verses five and six give two negative examples. On each occasion, the phrase underlines the author's previous point of why few Christians should become teachers too hastily. When controlled, the tongue can perform marvelous tasks, but left unchecked, the results can be catastrophic. Each analogy emphasizes control, and this is what James is emphasizing for the believer. Christians must learn to control their tongues.

The third sub-point is that inability to control the tongue reflects the character of the Christian, and this is supported by verses nine through twelve. Having just given four examples of control, James now moves to an analogy of lack of control. He flatly states this grotesque situation should not take place. By using the phrase "my brothers" (*adelphoi mou*) in the vocative case, James clearly addresses the church.[xvi] In renouncing this behavior, James uses the verb (*chre*) with the negative particle that should be translated "ought not." According to Craig Price, the sentence should be translated, as "These things ought not be so, my brothers."[xvii] James begins this section by explaining the incompatibility of a mouth from which both praises and curses come.[xviii] In emphasizing his point, James lists a series of analogies that reflects the unique state of fallen man:

> * Analogies reflecting disagreement
>   - Praises of God and curses of man (3:9)
>   - Can a fig tree produce grapes? (3:11)
>   - Can a grapevine produce figs? (3:12a)
>   - Can salt springs produce fresh water? (3:12b)

By bringing the tongue under control, the whole life can be guided into a life of well-doing. The point James is making in these verses is that believers who have not mastered the tongue are susceptible to some of the most grotesque perversions imaginable. This, once again, underscores his original point that believers should not seek too hastily to become teachers. We praise God, and then with the same mouth, we curse man who is created in the image of God. James does not see himself above this type of behavior, and this is reflected in the shift to "we" in verse nine. All Christians sin, but the one who can master the tongue draws near to perfection and reflects the *imago Dei*.

Christians reflect what we focus on in life. If we can learn to tame the tongue, we draw near to God and reflect his characteristics, but when we focus on the world, we reflect the characteristics of the world. Fig trees do not produce grapes; grapevines do not produce figs; saltwater streams do not produce fresh water, and the tongue of the Christian should not be used to curse man. The tongue was made to praise God, and when we curse man, we reflect the characteristics of the world.

Taming the Tongue:
Using Metaphor and Wisdom to Shape the Character of the Believer
James 3:1-12

INTRODUCTION
Literary Devices:
> The passage is framed by the phrase "my brothers" (*adelphoi mou*). These literary devices mark the beginning and ending points of the passage.

Organization of the passage:
> The passage is broken down by a series of metaphorical analogies about the tongue:
> * The Responsibility of the Teacher (3:1)
> * The Uncontrollable Tongue (3:2-8)
>   (1) Analogies of Size (3:2-5)
>   (2) Analogies of Force (3:6-8)
>   (3) Analogies of Incompatibility (3:9-12)

Main Point:
> The tongue is presented as the key to self-control for a virtuous life. By bringing the tongue under control, the whole self can be guided into well doing.

BODY
Sub-Points:
> **I. Christians should not aspire to become a teacher too hastily (3:1).**
>   A) Teaching is almost exclusively an oral form of communication. It is potentially dangerous and should be entered into with caution and reverence.
>   i. The verb translated as "become" (ginesthe) is a present imperative. In Greek, the imperative mood is used when making a command. Thus, believers are command not to aspire to become a teacher too hastily.
>   B) James separates the negative particle (not) from the verb (become) for emphasis.

        i. The negative imperative "not... should become" could imply to "stop becoming" and suggests that some in the congregation were using the position to attain status.
II. Christians must learn to control the tongue (3:2-8).
  A) There are a couple of literary devices that reflect that these verses should be interpreted together.
      i. The author uses a series of analogies that reflect both positive and negative uses of something small controlling something that is large:
      <u>Positive examples</u>
        * A small bit controlling a large horse (3:3)
        * A small rudder steering a large ship (3:4)
      <u>Negative examples</u>
        * A small tongue boasting of large accomplishments (3:5)
        * A small spark starting a large forest fire (3:6)
      ii. The phrase "the whole body" (*holon to soma*) is used three times in this passage (3:2, 3, and 6) to describe both positive and negative uses of the tongue.
      iii. Verses three and four give two positive examples of something small controlling something large, while verses five and six give two negative examples.
      iv. Each analogy emphasizes control, and this is what James is emphasizing for the believer.
      v. Believers must learn to control the tongue.
III. Inability to control the tongue reflects the character of the Christian (3:9-12).
  A) Having just given four examples of control, James now moves to an analogy of lack of control.
      i. By using the phrase "my brothers" (*adelphoi mou*) in the vocative case, James is addressing the church.
      ii. James begins this section by explaining the incompatibility of a mouth from which both praises and curses come (something that should not happen).
      iii. Analogies reflecting disagreement:
        - Praises of God and curses of man (3:9)
        - Can a fig tree produce grapes? (3:11)
        - Can a grapevine produce figs? (3:12a)
        - Can salt springs produce fresh water? (3:12b)

      iv. The point James is making in these verses is that believers who have not mastered the tongue are susceptible to some of the most grotesque perversions imaginable.

      v. Fig trees do not produce grapes; grapevines do not produce figs; saltwater streams do not produce fresh water, and the tongue of the Christian should not be used to curse man, who was made in God's image.

        * The tongue was made to praise God, and when we curse man, we reflect the characteristics of the world.

SUMMATION:

This is a passage that couples wisdom and speech, where the taming of the tongue is presented as the key to leading a virtuous life. As a result, Christians should not aspire too hastily to become teachers, since teaching requires maturity. In addition, teaching is almost exclusively an oral form of communication and is potentially dangerous for both the teacher and the student.

Final Thoughts:

This passage hinges on the ability of the pastor/teacher to recognize the uses of the metaphors. When controlled, the tongue can perform marvelous tasks, but left unchecked, the tongue can produce some of the most grotesque images of Christian behavior. By learning to tame the tongue, Christians are able to bring the whole of our lives into good behavior that reflects the image of God (*Imago Dei*).

---

[i] Fee and Stuart, *How to Read the Bible*, 400.

[ii] Martin Luther, *Prefaces to the New Testament*, (St. Louis: Concordia Publishing House, 2010), 10.

[iii] Kurt A. Richardson, *The New American Commentary: James*: (Nashville: Broadman & Holman Publishers, 1997), 145-46.

[iv] Dan McCartney, Baker *Exegetical Commentary:* James (Grand Rapids: Baker Books Publishing, 2009), 176.

[v] Craig L. Blomberg and Mariam J. Kamell, *Exegetical Commentary on the New Testament:* James, ed. by Clinton E. Arnold (Grand Rapids: Zondervan Publishing, 2008), 147. Blomberg and Karnell note that 1:5-8 and 1:19-26 pair speech and wisdom together.

[vi] Fee and Stewart, *How to Read*, 400.

[vii] Richardson, *James*, 145-60.

[viii] Ibid.

[ix] Ibid., 145.

[x] Ibid.

[xi] Blomberg and Kamell, *James*, 151.

[xii] Mounce, *Basics*, 310.

[xiii] Craig Price, *Biblical Exegesis of New Testament Greek:* James, (Eugene: Cascade Books, 2008), 105.

[xiv] Blomberg and Kamell, *James*, 151.

[xv] McCartney, *James*, 179.

[xvi] Mounce, *Basics*, 109-10. The vocative is the case of direct address.

[xvii] Price, *Biblical Exegesis*, 121.

[xviii] Richardson, *James*, 156-60.

Sermons that use the Psalter

David W. Brown

Chapter 14

Psalm 1
Commentary and Interpretation

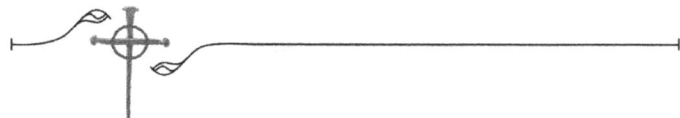

Great sermons encourage the believer to build a strong relationship with our Lord and thereby evaluate how we talk and pray to God. In his commentary on Psalms, John Goldingay wrote:

> How is the church to go about making such requests, praises, intercessions, and thanksgivings? And how are individuals or small groups to do that? The Bible assumes that we do not know instinctively how to talk with God but rather need some help with knowing how to do so.[i]

This is the purpose of the Psalter, and for centuries, believers have turned their attention to this book and their hearts to God. Sometimes, the authors have written with eloquence, and at other times with the jagged edges of a heart that had been broken. Yet the Psalter presents a rich mosaic of faith, pieced together across Israel's turbulent history, as its prayers and praises were laid before our Lord.

One of the characteristic features of the Psalms is the metaphorical language used throughout.[ii] Pastors have sometimes struggled to come to terms with this characteristic of the Psalter. In a 1997 article, poet and writer Kathleen Norris gave a blistering critique on the way pastors and theologians have failed to grasp this metaphorical use of language.[iii] She claimed that the church has failed to grasp what she termed as "incarnational language... words that resonate with the senses as they aim for the stars."[iv] Grasping these metaphorical relationships between the words and their meaning calls the reader to ponder God's Word at length. As William Brown noted, "To read theologically, is in part, to linger over the metaphor."[v]

Psalm 1 is considered a Torah psalm, and Old Testament scholars have typically come to view this psalm as a type of introductory psalm that describes the one who meditates upon the law as a paragon of faith.[vi] Goldingay claimed Psalm 1 was a poem that commented on how life worked.[vii] In addition, Psalm 1 contains a significant metaphor that is imperative for the pastor/teacher to grasp, the metaphor of pathway.[viii] This psalm metaphorically described the law as the way (*derekh*), or the path, to righteousness. In his book *Seeing the Psalms*, William Brown cited Psalm 119 as a classic example of the metaphor of pathway.[ix] Brown emphasized the metaphor of pathway when he wrote:

> How fortunate are those whose way (*derekh*) is blameless,
> > who walk in the law of YHWH.
> How fortunate are those who keep his decrees,
> > who seek him with their whole heart,
> > who also do no wrong,
> > [but] walk in his ways (*derekh*)[x]

Likewise, the author of Psalm 1 used the same Hebrew word (*derekh*)[xi] to metaphorically describe the same pathway. His emphasis was to contrast the one who lived on a path devoted to God with one who lived on the path of the sinner.[xii]

According to Peter Craigie and Marvin Tate, the structure of the psalm is set forth in three distinct parts that express the polarity of these two types of people and their destinies:[xiii]

> 1) The solid foundations of righteousness (1:1-3)
> 2) The impermanence of the wicked (1:4-5)
> 3) A contrast of the righteous and the wicked (1:6)[xiv]

Viewed as a whole, Psalm 1 does far more than simply give examples of what people should not do; the psalm reflects the state of people who have chosen paths that reflect how they live. Although the term Torah is used in verse one, Craigie and Tate argued that Torah should be viewed from the standpoint of instructions.[xv]

This leads to the main point of Psalm 1, and that is that this psalm reflects the contrasting paths of the righteous from the wicked by emphasizing the blessed state of living within the guidelines (*Torah*) set down by God. As noted earlier, the psalms in general reflect how believers talk to God and, thereby, build a strong relationship with him. Psalm 1 teaches that believers must give heed to God's instruction to find this blessing.[xvi] In other words, blessedness is not going to come about by itself; blessedness is given to those who commit themselves to living within the boundaries of God's paths.

The first sub-point of this psalm is the righteous do not live on a path of sin, and this is supported by verse one. The psalmist provides three parallel stages of a life the righteous are to avoid that progressively build to wrongdoing. Goldingay presented an excellent description of this pathway in his commentary:

> The basic form of wrongdoing involves simply action—"walking" by the advice of the faithless. Worse than that is "standing" in the path of moral failures, which implies more than simply taking that path but standing firm in it; the single action has become a way of life. Behind that is "sitting" in the "seat/session/company" of the mockers where sitting/dwelling (*yashov*) stands in parallelism with assembling/gathering (*moshav*). This implies not merely living their way but also taking part in their deliberations as they gather in a dark parody of the gathering of the elders at the city gate.[xvii]

Wrongdoing from this perspective reflects a path of progression that can be seen more clearly in the Septuagint (LXX) or the Greek translation of the Old Testament where the Greek verb "proceed" (*poreuomai*)[xviii] is used rather than walk (*peripateo*). A progression is the compositional pattern of logical, step-by-step, forward movement to an argument.[xix] Used in the context of Psalm 1, the term (*poreuomai*) reflects movement from one state (walking/standing/sitting) to another.

An example of this movement can be clearly seen in church life when an individual's attendance and commitment become sporadic and lead to a growing distance between the member and the church, and ultimately between the member and God. Left unchecked, the member will one day awaken only to find himself completely separated from God's path and wondering how he/she got himself into that situation. The point is that this circumstance did not come about all at once. It progressed from one state to another until they arrived at the final state.

The second sub-point is the righteous delight in God's instruction, and this is supported by verses two and three. The psalmist draws a contrast between the righteous and the wicked by claiming that the righteous delight in God's instruction (*Torah*). The law was designed to be a source of delight that was to be found only through regular meditation.[xx] They not only delight in God's instructions; they meditate on it. In verse three, the author used a simile to describe the righteous. A simile is a form of speech where one thing is likened to another using the word "like" or "as."[xxi] Craigie and Tate give a powerful analogy in their commentary:

> A tree may flourish or fade, depending on its location and access to water. A tree transplanted from a dry spot (e.g. wadi, where water runs only sporadically in the rainy season) to a location beside an irrigation channel, where water never ceases to flow, would inevitably flourish. It would become a green and fruitful tree.[xxii]

The author's analogy of a tree planted by streams of water is a vivid image of those who meditate on the law (*Torah*).[xxiii] Like the tree planted near streams of water, the believer whose life is planted in God's Word (*Torah*) will grow and flourish spiritually.

The third sub-point is the path of the righteous and the path of the wicked contrast one another, and this is supported by verses four through six. Just as the author used a simile to describe the path of the righteous, he follows this analogy with a contrasting simile that describes the path of the wicked. According to the psalmist, the wicked are like chaff. Craigie and Tate wrote that at harvest time, grain would be tossed into the air with a pitchfork over the threshing floor. When thrown into the air, the wind had a winnowing effect and would separate the chaff and blow it away, while the grain fell to the floor.[xxiv] This simile of the wicked is important to grasp because it describes the chaff as disappearing.

By coupling the two similes together in the psalm, the author draws an important contrast between the righteous and the wicked. Each path leads to an opposite direction in life. One leads to blessedness and delight while the other leads to disrepute and disappearance.[xxv] By using the metaphor of pathway and similes that vividly characterize the wicked and the righteous, the psalmist graphically contrasts the destiny of both.

David W. Brown

Torah, Metaphors, and Similes:
Using Literary Devices to Describe Two Paths in Life
Psalm 1

INTRODUCTION:

Metaphor:
> Psalm 1 uses the metaphor of pathway.

Literary feature from Psalm 119:
> The author of psalm 1 used the same Hebrew word (*derekh*) to metaphorically describe the pathway devoted to God.
> * How fortunate are those whose way (*derekh*) is blameless, who walk in the law of YHWH.
> * How fortunate are those who keep his decrees, who seek him with their whole heart, who also do no wrong, [but] walk in his ways (*derekh*).
> * The author of psalm 1 used the same Hebrew word (*derekh*) to metaphorically describe the same pathway devoted to God.

Characteristic Feature:
> Psalm 1 is considered a Torah psalm because of its emphasis in meditating upon the Torah.

Main Point:
> The psalm reflects the contrasting path of the righteous from the wicked by emphasizing the blessed state of living within the guidelines (*Torah*) set down by God.

BODY:

Sub-Points:
> **I. The righteous do not live on the path of sin (1:1).**
>> A) The psalmist provides three parallel stages of a life the righteous are to avoid that progressively build to wrongdoing.
>>> i. Wrongdoing can be seen as a progressive path in the LXX where the verb proceed (*poreuomai*) is used rather than the verb to walk (*peripateo*).
>>> ii. The verb "proceed" reflects movement from one state to another (walking/standing/sitting).

iii. Another example of this progressive movement can be seen in church life when an individual's attendance and commitment become sporadic and lead to a growing distance between the member and the church, and ultimately between the member and God.
iv. The point is that this circumstance did not come about all at once but progressed from one state to another until they arrived at the final state.

II. **The righteous delight in God's instruction (1:2-3).**
A) The psalmist draws a contrast between the righteous and the wicked by claiming that the righteous delight in God's instruction (*Torah*).
  i. The law was designed to be a source of delight that was to be found only through regular meditation. They not only delight in God's instructions; they meditate on it.
B) In verse three, the author used a simile to describe the righteous. A simile is a form of speech where one thing is likened to another using the word "like" or "as."
  i. The righteous are *like a tree* planted by streams of water is a vivid image of those who meditate on the Torah.

III. **The path of the righteous and the wicked contrast one another (1:4-6).**
A) Just as the author used a simile to describe the path of the righteous, he follows with a contrasting simile that describes the path of the wicked.
  i. According to the psalmist, the wicked are like chaff.
  ii. At harvest time, grain would be tossed into the air with a pitchfork over the threshing floor. When thrown into the air, the wind had a winnowing effect and would separate the chaff and blow it away, while the grain fell to the floor.
  iii. The simile of the wicked is important to grasp because it describes the chaff as disappearing.
B) By coupling the two similes together, the author draws an important contrast between the righteous and the wicked.
  i. Each path leads to an opposite direction in life. One leads to blessedness and delight, while the other leads to disrepute and disappearance.

C) By using the metaphor of pathway and similes that vividly characterize the wicked and the righteous, the psalmist vividly contrasts the destiny of both.

SUMMATION:

This is a psalm that contrasts the path of the righteous with the path of the wicked. The path we choose in life is crucial for both spiritual maturity and the character formation of the believer. The righteous delight in the meditation upon God's word, but the wicked refuse instruction.

Final Thoughts:

It is imperative the pastor/teacher recognize the metaphor of pathway, since the contrasting ways are based upon this imagery. These metaphorical references in this psalm shape the way the psalm is read, since every passage cannot be interpreted from a literal standpoint. Interpretation using metaphorical imagery does not mean the stories did not literally happen, but are simply a way to describe the substance of the story.

---

[i] John Goldingay, *Psalms*, vol. 1, 1-41 (Grand Rapids: Baker Academic Publishing, 2006), 22.

[ii] William P. Brown, Seeing the Psalms *the Psalms: A Theology of Metaphor* (Louisville: Westminster John Knox Press, 2002).

[iii] Kathleen Norris, "Incarnational Language" *Christian Century* 114/22 (July 30-August 6, 1997), 699.

[iv] Ibid.

[v] Brown, *Seeing the Psalms*, 13.

[vi] C. Hassell Bullock, *Encountering the Book of Psalms: A Literary and Theological Introduction* (Grand Rapids: Baker Academic Publishing, 2001), 59.

[vii] Goldingay, *Psalms*, 80.

[viii] Brown, *Seeing the Psalms*, 31-54.

[ix] Ibid., 32.

[x] Ibid.

[xi] Pratico and Van Pelt, *Basics*, 36.

[xii]Goldingay, *Psalms*, 83.

[xiii]Peter C. Craigie and Marvin E. Tate, *Word Biblical Commentary*, Psalms 1-50, vol. 19, Second Edition (Nashville: Thomas Nelson Publishers, 2004), 59.

[xiv]Ibid., 59.

[xv]Ibid., 61.

[xvi]Goldingay, *Psalms*, 91.

[xvii]Ibid., 82.

[xviii]Bernard A. Taylor, *Analytical Lexicon to the Septuagint*: Expanded Edition (Peabody: Hendrickson Publishers Marketing, 2009), 231. Eporeuthe is the aorist passive form of poreuomai.

[xix]Kendell H. Easley, *User-Friendly Greek: A Common Sense Approach to the Greek New Testament* (Nashville: Broadman & Holman Publishing, 1994), 164. I am applying this concept to the LXX pattern.

[xx]Craigie and Tate, *Word*, 60.

[xxi]J.A. Cuddon and C.E. Preston, *The Dictionary of Literary Terms and Literary Theory*: Fourth Edition (London: Penguin Publishing, 2000), 830.

[xxii]Craigie and Tate, *Word*, 60.

[xxiii]Bullock, *Encountering*, 219.

[xxiv]Craigie and Tate, *Psalms*, 61.

[xv]Bullock, *Encountering*, 219.

David W. Brown

Chapter 15

Psalm 19
Commentary and Interpretation

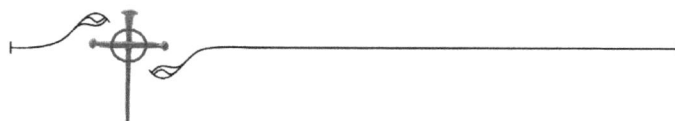

Great sermons link together imagery that enhances the believer's understanding of a particular passage. They tie together metaphorical images that illuminate our understanding of Scripture, and when these vivid images are recognized, they fuel the believer's desire to know and understand God in a deeper way. Psalm 19 helps pastor/teachers accomplish this task.

C.S. Lewis considered this psalm to be one of the greatest poems of the Psalter and its lyrics to be some of the greatest in the world,[i] and William P. Brown claimed in his book *Seeing the Psalms* that this psalm is a poetic tour de force that brings together image and word and gives witness to the explosive reaction that ensues.[ii] Both of these scholars recognized the beauty of grasping the metaphorical images Psalm 19 uses to describe the illuminating impact upon man. Also, Old Testament scholars classify this psalm as a wisdom psalm because of its use of wisdom ideas and terminology that is considered to be wisdom vocabulary.[iii]

Psalm 19 uses the metaphor of the sun to graphically describe God's Word. The catalyst that drives this metaphor is the concept of illumination. Just as the sun illuminates the heavens, God's word (*Torah*) illuminates the believer. This metaphor is so instrumental to the interpretation of this psalm that every illustration in the psalm hinges upon this literary device. Therefore, the importance of grasping this metaphor cannot be over stated.

The structure of this psalm also reflects a repeated emphasis on illumination, which can be seen below:

God's Illuminating Handiwork (19:1-3)
  1. Heavens – The dwelling place of the sun (19:1)
  2. Day and Night – The course of a 24-hour day (19:2)
  3. Emanating Radiance of Speech (19:3)

The Sun's Illumination (19:4-6)
  1. Tent – The dwelling place of the sun (v4b)
  2. Strong Man – Running his course (19:5)
  3. Emanating Radiance of the Sun (19:6b)

The Torah's Illumination to Man (19:7-9)
  - Laws and precepts for living a life that honors God

The Blessings of Being Illuminated (19:10-14)
  - Rewards for keeping God's word[iv]

There is also a literary movement within the psalm that moves the reader from the general to the specific. The movement can be seen below:

* From God (19:1) to Lord (19:7)
* From general knowledge (9:2) to divine instruction (19:7)
* From natural illumination [specifically the sun] (19:5) to divine illumination [specifically the Torah] (19:7)

All of these literary movements are designed to lead the reader to grasp the significance of God's divine illumination found in his Word.

One other illustration serves to emphasize the importance of divine illumination. The psalmist goes to great lengths to chart the path of the sun, and the believer is destined to an even more detailed path when he follows the Torah.

* The sun's path rises from one end of the heavens to the other (19:6)
* The benefits of the sun's path: pours forth speech in the daytime and reveals knowledge at night (19:2)

Likewise:
* God's path rises from his word, testimony, precepts, commandments, fear, and judgments (19:7-9)
* The benefits of God's path: Restores the soul, makes the simple

> wise, causes the heart to rejoice, endures forever, and are righteous all together (19:10-13)[v]

God's path is far more detailed than the path of the sun, and the benefits also far out-weigh the general knowledge of God through nature. In a similar fashion, D. J. A. Clines argued persuasively that each of the characteristics of the Torah contains an illusion to the tree of knowledge in the Garden of Eden.[vi] His point followed a general to specific movement, where divine wisdom that was derived from the Torah was superior to the tree of knowledge (general knowledge) in Genesis 2-3. While the sun illuminates the heavens, an even greater illumination comes about when believers study God's Word and keep it in their hearts. This leads to the main point, and that is the psalmist uses the metaphor of the sun to vividly describe the illuminating effects of God's Word (*Torah*) upon believers.

The first sub-point is the psalmist uses the metaphor of the sun to describe God's illuminating work, and this is supported by verses one through six. The metaphor of the sun has already been noted, but the psalmist's point is to illuminate God's work. The reader of the psalm makes this point in verse one. God's illuminating work is emphasized first through a grammatical nuance. Brown noted that the verb "pour forth" (*yabbia*) literally means "to gush"[vii] and is better portrayed as a geyser gushing forth streams of water. In the context of Psalm 19, however, the sun's illumination is described as radiant lines that often emanate from behind a dark cloud. The emanating rays of light are not heard but seen. As a pastor, I have often noted that sometimes, the beauty of God's Word follows the same path. Some of the most beautiful illustrations can only be read in the original language. I can tell the congregation about the beauty of a chiastic structure or Hebrew parallelism, but sometimes, the beauty of these illustrations cannot be heard, but only beheld. As a result, my greatest illustrations of God's Word in sermon proclamation sometimes fall short when expressed verbally.

The second sub-point is the psalmist teaches that God illuminates man through his Word, and this is supported by verses seven through nine. The movement from the heavens (19:1) to the Torah (19:7) to humanity/his servant (19:11) is crucial for the pastor to recognize because it teaches mankind that humanity has a place in God's universal scheme of things.[viii] While the sun illuminates the heavens and the beauty of God's work, the climax of God's work is emphasized by enlightening mankind to God's will through instruction (*Torah*). As Peter Craigie and Marvin Tate noted, by making the simple wise, God provides wisdom, without which life would culminate in the disasters of folly.[ix] Charles Swindoll beautifully summarized the emphasis on instruction and illumination in a poignant story by Loyd Cory:

> A number of years ago, there appeared in the New Yorker magazine an account of a Long Island resident who ordered an extremely sensitive barometer from a respected company, Abercrombie and Fitch. When the instrument arrived at his home, he was disappointed to discover that the indicating needle appeared to be stuck pointing to the sector marked "Hurricane." After shaking the barometer vigorously several times—never a good idea with a sensitive mechanism—and never getting the point to move, the new owner wrote a scathing letter to the store, and, on the following morning, on the way to his New York office he mailed it. That evening, he returned to Long Island to find not only the barometer missing, but his house as well! The needle of the instrument had been pointing correctly. The month was September; the year was 1938, the day of the terrible hurricane that almost leveled Long Island.[x]

The point is that failure to be illuminated or to follow instruction often brings calamity to our lives, and this is what happens when humanity fails to be illuminated and follow God's instructions. Adam and Eve are classic examples of this colossal failure. They failed to be illuminated by God's teaching, and as a result, suffered the consequences for their failure. [xi]

The third sub-point is the psalmist describes the benefits of keeping God's word, and this is supported by verses ten through fourteen. In verse ten, the psalmist goes to great lengths to illustrate the benefits of keeping God's word. As Brown noted, "the abrupt change in imagery from gold's luster to honey's sweetness in the psalm suggests a deliberate shift from sight to taste, indicating the individual's appropriation of authoritative teaching."[xii] The idea here is that through the illumination of God's Word, the psalmist is able to identify sinful behavior that would normally go undetectable by the human will, and this is a great benefit for the believer.[xiii]

Throughout this passage, the psalmist metaphorically describes the impact that God's Word has upon those who meditate upon it (*Torah*). He will illuminate his people in a greater way than the sun illuminates the heavens. When we meditate upon his Word, God will illuminate his path and opens our eyes to the greatness of his presence.

Moving from the Sun to the Law:
A Psalm of Metaphor and Illumination
Psalm 19

INTRODUCTION:
Literary Devices:
Psalm 19 uses the metaphor of the sun to vividly describe God's word. The catalyst that drives this metaphor is the concept of illumination. Just as the sun illuminates the heavens, God's Word (*Torah*) illuminates the believer.

Structure of the Psalm:
The structure of this psalm also reflects a repeated emphasis on illumination and can be seen below:
* God's Illuminating Handiwork (19:1-3)
    1. Heavens – The dwelling place of the sun (19:1)
    2. Day and Night – The course of a 24-hour day (19:2)
    3. Emanating Radiance of Speech (19:3)
* Sun's Illumination (19:4-6)
    1. Tent – The dwelling place of the sun (19:4b)
    2. Strong Man – Running his course (19:5)
    3. Emanating Radiance of the Sun (19:6b)
* Torah Illumination (19:7-9)
    - Laws and precepts for living a life that honors God
* Blessings of Being Illuminated (19:10-14)
    - Rewards for keeping God's word

Literary Movements:
* From God (19:1) to Lord (19:7)
* From general knowledge (19:2) to divine instruction (19:7)
* From natural illumination [specifically the sun] (19:5) to divine illumination [specifically the Torah] (19:7)

Main Point:
The psalmist uses the metaphor of the sun to describe the illuminating effects of God word (*Torah*) upon believers.

Examples of Divine Illumination:
  * The sun's path rises from one end of the heavens to the other (19:6)
  * The benefits of the sun's path: pours forth speech in the daytime and reveals knowledge at night (19:2)

Likewise:
  * God's path rises from his word, testimony, precepts, commandments, fear, and judgments (19:7-9)
  * The benefits of God's path: Restores the soul, makes the simple wise, causes the heart to rejoice, endures forever, and are righteous all together (19:10-13)

BODY:
Sub-Points

I. **The psalmist uses the metaphor of the sun to describe God's illuminating work (19:1-6).**
   A) The psalmist's point is to illuminate God's work.
      i. God's illuminating work is emphasized first through a grammatical nuance.
      ii. The verb "pour forth" (*yabbia*) literally means "to gush," and is better portrayed as a geyser gushing forth streams of water.
      iii. In the context of Psalm 19, the sun's illumination is described as radiant lines that often emanate from behind a dark cloud. The emanating rays of light are not heard, but seen.

II. **The psalmist teaches that God illuminates man through his Word (19:7-9).**
   A) The movement from the heavens (19:1) to the Torah (19:7) to humanity/his servant (19:11) is crucial for the pastor/teacher to recognize because it teaches mankind that humanity has a place in God's universal scheme of things.
      i. While the sun illuminates the heavens and the beauty of God's work, the climax of God's work is emphasized by enlightening mankind to God's will through instruction (*Torah*).
      ii. By making the simple wise, God provides wisdom without which life would culminate in the disasters of folly.

Illustration:
> "A number of years ago, there appeared in the *New Yorker* magazine an account of a Long Island resident who ordered an extremely sensitive barometer, from a respected company, Abercrombie and Fitch. When the instrument arrived at his home he was disappointed to discover that the indicating needle appeared to be stuck pointing to the sector marked "Hurricane." After shaking the barometer vigorously several times—never a good idea with a sensitive mechanism—and never getting the point to move, the new owner wrote a scathing letter to the store, and, on the following morning, on the way to his New York office, he mailed it. That evening, he returned to Long Island to find not only the barometer missing, but his house as well! The needle of the instrument had been pointing correctly. The month was September; the year was 1938, the day of the terrible hurricane that almost leveled Long Island."

 III. **The psalmist describes the benefits of keeping God's Word (19:10-14).**
  A) The abrupt change in imagery from gold's luster to honey's sweetness in the psalm suggests a deliberate shift from sight to taste, indicating the individual's appropriation of authoritative teaching.
   i. The idea here is that through the illumination of God's Word, the psalmist is able to identify sinful behavior that would normally go undetectable by the human will, and this is a great benefit for the believer.

SUMMATION:
This is a psalm that uses the metaphor of the sun to vividly describe the illuminating effects God's word has upon the believer. Just as the sun illuminates the heavens, so God's Word illuminates believers.

Final Thoughts:
Grasping the metaphor of the sun is crucial for the interpretation of this Psalm. This metaphor is so instrumental to the interpretation of this psalm that every illustration in the psalm hinges upon this literary device.

[i] C.S. Lewis, *Reflections on the Psalms* (New York: Harvest Book/Harcourt Publishing, 1958), 63.

[ii] Brown, *Seeing the Psalms*, 103.

[iii] Bullock, *Encountering*, 204. See also Craige and Tate, *Psalms*, 180.

[iv] Brown, *Seeing the Psalms*, 83. The structure was taken from William Brown's outline and changed to reflect the illumination that he beautifully articulated in chapter 4 of his book.

[v] Ibid., 85. Brown's emphasis is that God's word illuminates man in a much greater way than the sun illuminates the heavens.

[vi] D.J.A. Clines "The Tree of Knowledge and the Law of Yahweh" in *Vetus Testamentum* 24 [1974] p. 8-14.

[vii] Brown, *Seeing the Psalms*, 83.

[viii] Craigie and Tate, *Psalms*, 183.

[ix] Ibid.

[x] Loyd Cory, *Quote Unquote*, 347. As summarized in Charles Swindoll's *Ultimate Book of Illustrations & Quotes: Over 1,500 Outstanding Ways to Effectively Drive Home Your Message* (Nashville: Thomas Nelson Publishers, 1998), 593.

[xi] Goldingay, *Psalms*, vol. 1, 293.

[xii] Brown, *Seeing the Psalms*, 243. See footnote 100.

[xiii] John Ker, *The Psalms in History and Biography* (Eidenburgh: Andrew Elliot Printing, 1888), 143.

[xiv] Ibid., 85. Brown's emphasis is that God's word illuminates man in a much greater way than the sun illuminates the heavens.

David W. Brown

Chapter 16

Psalm 23
Commentary and Interpretation

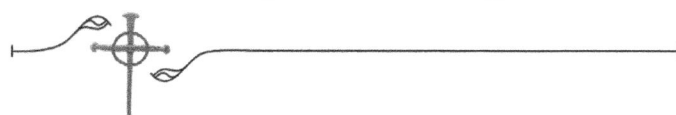

Great sermons emphasize the beauty and poetic nature of the Scripture. The twenty-third psalm is one of the most beautiful psalms in the Bible, especially when read from the KJV translation. This psalm is considered by Old Testament scholars to be a psalm of trust, and this type of psalm can share several unique literary features. According to C. Hassell Bullock, psalms of trust bore the hearts of the ancient worshipers and revealed the spiritual buoys that kept them afloat amidst their world of pain and turmoil.[i] In modern times, the twenty-third psalm has come to be associated with funerals and death, but as J. Clinton McCann mentioned, this psalm is actually a psalm that is about living and puts activities such as eating, drinking, and seeking security in God as the center point of faith.[ii]

The organization of this psalm is quite significant for interpretational purposes, and two points should be noted. First, the psalm begins (23:1) and ends (23:6) with the word "Lord" (*Yahweh*) and forms a literary *inclusio* over the entire psalm. Thus, the psalm is framed by the word *Yahweh*. Literary devices that frame a passage with a repeated word commonly function as a type of bookend to the passage. As a result, the *inclusio* places the Lord at both the beginning and the end of a psalm that describes life metaphorically to be a spiritual pilgrimage from the shepherd's field to the house of the Lord.

Second, while there is much debate about the interpretation of this psalm, there is some consensus that the psalm is divided into two parts:[iii]

> * Verses 1-4 portray the Lord (*Yahweh*) as a shepherd and list his protection.
> * Verses 5-6 portray the Lord (*Yahweh*) as a host and list his provisions.

The structure of the psalm is important to recognize, since it highlights three significant literary movements that anchor the psalm and influence how it is to be interpreted. These movements are listed below:

> 1. The movement from shepherd to host[iv]
> 2. The movement from protection to provision[v]
> 3. The movement from the field of the shepherd to the house of the Lord[vi]

In addition, the twenty-third Psalm is a psalm that uses the metaphor of pathway (23:3), but as William Brown noted, the connection between "pathway" and "refuge" are integrally related.[vii] In a 1982 article, Rueben Ahroni agreed with the metaphorical use of "pathway" but claimed the tranquil pathway was deceptive. He wrote:

> It is no accident that the one who is led in the "paths of righteousness" is also the one who traverses the "darkest valley" and resolves, "to dwell in the house of YHWH." For all its pastoral imagery, the so called Shepherd Psalm charts the harrowing journey of an individual pursued by unnamed enemies yet led and protected by God.[viii]

These literary structures and movements clearly influence the interpretation of this psalm and lead to the main point: the twenty-third psalm is a psalm of trust where David encourages the reader to place his/her whole life in the loving care of the divine shepherd (*Yahweh*) who protects, restores, provides, and guides believers through life.

The first sub-point is God is our Shepherd and our Protector, and this is supported by verses one through four. According to Peter Craigie and Marvin Tate, the first four verses contain an extended metaphor: God is the shepherd, and the psalmist is one of the sheep belonging to his flock.[ix] The shepherd's role was to provide food, water, and protection for the sheep, and that requirement forced the shepherd into being a strong character. As a result, the shepherd imagery is also an image of strength and power that is attributed to God,[x] and much of the imagery comes from Isaiah, who wrote, "Like a shepherd, he will tend his flock, in his arm, he will gather the lambs and carry them in his bosom; he will gently lead the nursing ewes (Isaiah 40:11)."

Christians in North America often portray the image of the shepherd as a father figure, but as the *Midrash on Psalms* pointed out, the occupation of shepherding was not always a gentle, pastoral one, but was often viewed as a despised occupation.[xi] David pointed out to Saul that shepherds were rough and tough characters who need to be brave if they are going to protect the sheep from threats (1 Sam. 17:34-36).[xii] In addition, sheep are wandering animals constantly seeking food and protection, so as John Goldingay pointed out, for sheep to lie down rather than simply to feed suggests ample provisions and protection.[xiii]

Craigie and Tate also claimed that verses one through four reflect the Lord's protection while, at the same time, they reflect the wilderness generation's travels following the exodus.[xiv] They noted the Hebrew verb for not "lacking" (*chsr*) in verse one is the same verb used in Deuteronomy 2:7, and this shared verb reflected the imagery of the exodus background.[xv] The linkage to Deuteronomy also extends the metaphor of the shepherd by conjuring up the imagery of a shepherd in the wilderness. The Palestinian shepherd normally carried two implements: a club (or rod) to fend off wild beasts and a crook (or staff) to guide and control the sheep.[xvi] All of this imagery is used to describe the Lord as both a shepherd and a protector. The Lord is a God who leads believers through deep valleys of darkness through life. The reason for confidence in the Lord is found in his protection and is metaphorically described by the shepherd's rod and staff used as a description of power.[xvii]

The second sub-point is that God is our gracious host and provider, and this point is supported by verse five. The literary movement from shepherd to host has already been noted, but the ample provisions by the Lord/host are significant. In the ancient world, to set a table for someone and provide wine was the act of a gracious and wise host (Proverbs 9:1-2). According to Longman, this was considered to be an act of celebration and compliments the host of the banquet.[xviii] The Hebrew noun translated as "overflows" (*rewaya*) describes abundance to the point of saturation. This rare word is used only on two occasions in the Old Testament,[xix] and these gracious actions describe the goodness of our Lord. In addition, the literary movement from shepherd to host is crucial for interpretational purposes, since the transition encompasses the imagery of both shepherd/protector as well as a host/provider. All of this imagery and grammar describes God as a gracious host who provides for his people.

The third sub-point is that God pursues his people, and this is supported by verse six. Nearly all English translations of the Bible translate the Hebrew verb *yirdefu* as "to follow," but the verb also means "to pursue."[xx] In the context of this psalm, the verb is used in an imperfect conjugation that Gary Pratico and Miles Van Pelt pointed out can be used to denote habitual or customary action.[xxi] The significance of this verb cannot be overestimated, as it teaches believers a crucial aspect about the character of our Lord. God does not just hope we follow his paths; he pursues us. He chases after his people so we will continue to follow his paths of righteousness. Goldingay made an excellent point when he wrote that the verb "pursue" carries two encouraging implications.[xxii] First, if wild animals/enemies (23:1-5) pursue us, God's goodness and mercy do as well.[xxiii] The second point was that goodness and mercy pursue us with energy.[xxiv] Our Lord is not a lethargic God sitting in Heaven hoping that believers follow his paths. He pursues us with vigor.

In 2005, my wife and I were forced to evacuate and flee a coming hurricane that set its sights upon the city of New Orleans. We had lived in New Orleans for five years and had come to see evacuations as somewhat routine, but the aftermath of *Hurricane Katrina* was far worse than anyone could have imaged. Having lost everything we owned, the Katrina event became a turning point in our lives as we sought by faith to focus on our Lord for direction. There were two points that we learned from the Katrina catastrophe:

First, the Lord's path may not be a path of our choosing. We would have certainly chosen another path if it were up to us, but even in the midst of our difficulties and frustrations, the Lord blessed us immensely by teaching us what was truly important in life. Significance was not found in furniture, clothes, or personal possessions. Rather, significance was having a Lord who pursued us and reached down from Heaven, scooped us up out of a valley of death, delivered us safely to a place of his choosing, and told us to "minister there."

Second, if we learned nothing else, it was what it means to persevere in the faith. We had both good days and bad, but through them all, our

Lord taught us to be faithful to him through difficult circumstances. We were not unique to the sufferings of *Hurricane Katrina*, but this was the pathway of his choosing, and it is a path that leads to his home where we will one day dwell with him forever.

The twenty-third psalm is a psalm that teaches believers to trust in our Lord. He is the bookend to a life of both tragedy and goodness as he protects, guides, and pursues us throughout our lives.

David W. Brown

The Lord as Shepherd and Host:
Looking to God as our Protector, Guide, and Restorer
Psalm 23

INTRODUCTION:
Organization of the Psalm:
> * Verses 1-4 portray the Lord (*Yahweh*) as a shepherd and list his protection.
> * Verses 5-6 portray the Lord (*Yahweh*) as a host and list his provisions.

Structure of the Psalm:
> The psalm begins (23:1) and ends (23:6) with the word "Lord" (*Yahweh*) and forms a literary *inclusio* over the entire psalm.

Literary Movements:
> The structure of the psalm is important to recognize, since it highlights three significant literary movements that anchors the psalm and influences how it is to be interpreted:
> 1. The movement from shepherd to host
> 2. The movement from protection to provision
> 3. The movement from the field of the shepherd to the house of the Lord

Main Point:
> The twenty-third psalm is a psalm of trust, where David encourages the reader to place his/her whole life in the loving care of the divine shepherd (*Yahweh*) who protects, restores, provides, and guides believers through life.

BODY:
Sub-Points:
> I. God is our shepherd and our protector (23:1-4).
>> A) The first four verses contain an extended metaphor: God is the shepherd, and the psalmist is one of the sheep belonging to his flock.

i. The shepherd's role was to provide food, water, and protection for the sheep, and that requirement forced the shepherd into being a strong character.
   ii. The shepherd imagery is borrowed from Isaiah 40:11, "Like a shepherd, he will tend his flock; in his arm, he will gather the lambs and carry them in his bosom; he will gently lead the nursing ewes."
   iii. Sheep are wandering animals, constantly seeking food and protection, so for sheep to lie down rather than simply to feed suggests ample provisions and protection.
  B) Verses one through four reflect the Lord's protection, while at the same time, reflect the wilderness generation's travels following the exodus.
   i. The Hebrew verb for not "lacking" (*chsr*) in verse one is the same verb used in Deuteronomy 2:7 and this shared verb reflects the imagery of the exodus background.
II. **God is our gracious host and provider (23:5).**
  A) In the ancient world, to set a table for someone and provide wine was the act of a gracious and wise host (Proverbs 9:1-2).
   i. The Hebrew noun translated as "overflows" (*rewaya*) describes abundance to the point of saturation.
   ii. This rare word is used only on two occasions in the Old Testament, and these gracious actions describe the goodness of our Lord.
  B) The literary movement from shepherd to host is crucial for interpretational purposes, since the transition encompasses the imagery of both shepherd/protector as well as a host/provider.
   i. All of this imagery and grammar describes God as a gracious host who provides for his people.
III. **God pursues his people (23:6).**
  A) Virtually all English translations of the Bible translate the Hebrew verb (*yirdefu*) as "to follow," but the verb also means "to pursue."
   i. In the context of this psalm, the verb is used in an imperfect conjugation used to denote habitual or customary action.
   ii. The significance of this verb cannot be overestimated, as it teaches believers a crucial aspect about the character of our Lord.

        iii. God does not just hope we follow his paths; he pursues us. He chases after his people so they will continue to follow his paths of righteousness.

SUMMATION:

The twenty-third psalm is a psalm of trust, in which David encourages the reader to place his/her whole life in the loving care of the divine shepherd (*Yahweh*) who protects, restores, provides, and guides believers through life. Our Lord is not a lethargic God sitting in Heaven hoping that believers follow his paths. He pursues us with vigor.

Final Thoughts:

The metaphors in this psalm, as well as the literary movements, are crucial for proper interpretation, since they provide striking imagery of God as protector, as well as God as a host. In addition, the Hebrew verb "to pursue" in verse six offers a vivid illustration of a loving God who chases after those he loves to keep them upon his path.

---

[i] Bullock, *Encountering*, 168.

[ii] J. Clinton McCann, *New Interpreter's Bible, Psalms*, Vol. 4 (Nashville: Abington Press, 1996), 767.

[iii] Craigie and Tate, *Psalms*, 204.

[iv] Ibid, 204-05.

[v] Ibid.

[vi] Bullock, *Encountering*, 171.

[vii] Brown, *Psalms*, 40.

[viii] Rueben Ahroni, "The Unity of Psalm 23" in the *Hebrew Annual Review* 6 [1982]: 21-34.

[ix] Craigie and Tate, *Psalms*, 205.

[x] Goldingay, *Psalms*, 348.

[xi] William G. Braude, *The Midrash on Psalms:* Yale Judaica Series, Vol. 13 (New Haven: Yale University Press, 1959), 327.

[xii] Goldingay, *Psalms*, 348.

[xiii] Ibid., 349-51.

[xiv] Craigie and Tate, *Psalms*, 206.

[xv] Ibid.

[xvi] Ibid.

[xvii] Ibid., 207.

[xviii] Tremper Longman III, *Baker Commentary on the Old Testament Wisdom and Psalms: Proverbs* (Grand Rapids: Baker Academic Publishing, 2006.), 216.

[xix] The noun *rewaya* is used only in Psalms 23:5 and 66:12.

[xx] Pratico and Van Pelt, *Basics*, 257.

[xxi] Ibid., 166.

[xxii] Goldingay, *Psalms*, 352.

[xxiii] Ibid.

[xxiv] Ibid.

David W. Brown

Chapter 17

Psalm 42 - 43
Commentary and Interpretation

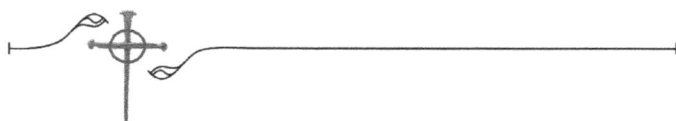

Great sermons bring hope to those in need and invigorate those who have been worn down by life. Over the years, visiting the homebound has become one of my favorite activities. It is a ministry that inspires and lifts my heart when I am feeling low. In some churches, the homebound can be forgotten because of the staff's busy schedules, but I look forward to my visitation day each week. One reason this ministry touches my heart so much is the grateful attitudes of those I visit. Our homebound talk frequently of the "good old days," and for them, those days were when they could come to church. They were days of singing and fellowship, and the fondness of these days is remembered with smiles on their faces and a twinkle in their eyes.

Literary devices play a major role for interpreting this psalm. Gordon Fee and Douglas Stuart noted a couple of literary devices that indicate that Psalms 42 and 43 should be interpreted together.[i] First, both psalms speak of their souls being in despair (42:5 and 11, 43:5). Second, there is a repeated strophe in these psalms that suggests they should be interpreted together. The strophe was a Greek term associated with a choral ode in a Greek drama,[ii] but over time, it came to be used as a structural division of a poem containing stanzas of varying line-length.[iii] The strophe in these two psalms is easily recognizable:

* Hope in God, for I shall again praise him (42:5).
* Hope in God, for I shall again praise him (42:11).
* Hope in God, for I shall again praise him (43:5).

In addition, Tremper Longman and Raymond Dillard noted that by combining Psalm 43 with the interpretation of Psalm 42 unites a recurring refrain previously established in Psalm 42:[iv]

* (a) Lament (42:2-5)
* (b) *Refrain* (42:6)
* (a) Lament (42:7-11)
* (b) *Refrain* (42:12)
* (a) Prayer (43:1-4)
* (b) *Refrain* (43:6)[v]

Peter Craigie and Marvin Tate noted the structure moves the psalmist from near despair to surging confidence,[vi] while John Goldingay claimed that together, the structure of the psalms produces a balance between lament/plea and looking to the future.[vii] The compounding effect of all these literary features indicates that these two psalms should be interpreted together.

The structure of the psalm proposed by Craigie and Tate is crucial from an interpretational standpoint since Psalm 43 provides a fitting conclusion to the predicament given in Psalm 42. In addition, the structure reflects a movement from despair to joy that anchors the interpretation of the passage. These movements can be seen below:

* From a soul that thirsts for God (42:2) to one that praises God (43:4)
* From being led by memories (42:4) to being led God's light and truth (43:3)
* From processions at the house of God (42:4) to his alter (43:4)

In addition, William Brown noted that "flowing streams" are associated with Zion, the "house of God (v4)," so the image of the thirsty deer conveys most vividly the psalmist's singular yearning for God.[viii] The psalmist inundates the reader with repetitive images of gushing water to vividly describe his life as it ebbs and flows with the presence of God.[ix] Sometimes the psalmist's faith runs dry, but it will surely roar again with a vengeance of God's supplying power.[x] The imagery can be seen below:

* A deer panting for water brooks (42:1)
* A soul thirsting for God (42:2)
* Souls being poured out (42:4)
* The sound of God's waterfalls (42:7)
* Waves rolling over the psalmist (42:7)

All of these metaphors of water ebbing, flowing, and gushing reflect movements in our faith that range from despair to hope. Faith, unfortunately, does not consist of moving from one spiritual peak to another, but rather, faith ebbs and flows like these metaphorical water references. If believers are going to stay afloat during trials in life, we must place our faith upon God who sustains, rather than placing our faith in troubles that plague us in life. This leads to the main point of the passage, and that is when believers turn from memories that plague our past to God who sustains, we take the first step on a path that leads from a soul in despair to one with exceeding joy.

The first sub-point is the psalmist's memories of the past led him into despair, and this sub-point is supported by verses one through five. The psalmist's overwhelming desire is to get to the temple. He remembers back to a time of participation in worship, but for some unknown reason, is no longer able to do so. Verses one and two speak of a soul longing for God using the simile of a deer that pants for water in a like manner. The Hebrew verb (*ta'arog*) translated "to long for" is a Hebrew imperfect. The imperfect tense is typically used to express an incomplete action, but is also is used to denote a habitual action.[xi] The idea being expressed is that just as a thirsty deer habitually longs for water, so the psalmist's thirsty soul habitually longs for God. Our homebound often share with me their memories of bygone days when they stood in the sanctuary of the church and felt the greatness of God's presence. The longing they experience reflects the same imagery of the psalmist's soul in despair.

The second sub-point is the psalmist moves from worldly references to heavenly references, and this is supported by verse six. A spiritually mature believer does not focus on worldly problems because those problems can bring a soul into despair. Like an internal memo in the business world that contains a "from" and "to" reference, the same shift is made in the passage from where the psalmist's thoughts originally began to where they ended. The literary shift can be seen below:

From:
* The land of the Jordan (42:6)
* The peaks of Hermon (42:6)
* Mount Mizar (42:6)

To:
- Your holy hill (43:3)
- Your dwelling places (43:3)
- The alter of God (43:3)

These literary movements reflect a shift in the psalmist's thoughts as he moves from thinking of himself and the problems that plague him/her to thinking of God and the solution. Craigie and Tate's comment reflected the same concept when they wrote:

> When the psalmist stops speaking to himself (Ps 42) and addresses his words to God (Ps 43), the beginning of his deliverance is in sight. And again, the literary structure may reveal the solution for reality; when one turns from the memories and the burdens within the mind and boldly addresses to God a plea for deliverance, the first step is taken on the path that leads ultimately to a restoration of the life of praise and to mental and spiritual health.[xii]

The third sub-point is the psalmist moves from despair to restoration, and this is supported by Psalm 43 verse five. The psalmist noted repeatedly his antagonists (42:9, 43:1) and their repeated bombardment of hurtful questioning. Have you ever been depressed with circumstances in life and begin to think about people who have made you angry? Maybe you were hurt by their comments that infuriated you and this seemed to compound the problem as it moved from bad to worse. Over time, we come to see these people as our enemies who have contributed to our demise. William Brown described the same scenario when he wrote:

> The psalmist, moreover, feels hunted and mortally wounded by the verbal barbs of his detractors in their relentless questioning: "Where is your God?" (42:3,10). The enemies deadliest weapon, as noted in other psalms, is their discourse; their questions shoot forth like arrows that pierce everything that defined and nurtured the psalmist's very being or "soul" (vv4-5,11). The figure of the doe thus lends a poignant sense of pathos, as well as a humble piety, to the profile of the speaker.[xiii]

The psalmist is using this rhetoric to make an important point. He is not trivializing problems in life and simply telling us to have positive thoughts; rather, he recognizes the hurtful force expressed in derogatory statements and encourages the reader to focus on the one who can solve these problems.

As vivid and hurtful as these comments are, they also provide a starting point to a rhetorical transition that moves from focusing on problems in life to focusing on God. The transition moves from a soul in despair (42:5, 11) to a soul of exceeding joy praising God (43:4) and from being led by his memories (42:4) to being led by God's light and truth (43:3). By applying the psalmist's principles expressed in these two psalms, the pastor can instruct believers to shift their focus from worldly problems to Godly solutions. And by doing so, we can encourage our homebound church members by reminding them that "the good old days" are not behind us but in front of us.

David W. Brown

Moving From Despair to Restoration:
A Psalm for the Frail and the Homebound
Psalm 42:1-43:5

INTRODUCTION
Literary Devices:
>There are a couple of literary devices that indicate that Psalms 42 and 43 should be interpreted together:
> 1. Both psalms speak of their souls being in despair (42:5, 11, 43:5).
> 2. The repeated strophe in these psalms suggests the two psalms should be interpreted together:
>   * Hope in God for I shall again praise him (42:5)
>   * Hope in God for I shall again praise him (42:11)
>   * Hope in God for I shall again praise him (43:5)

Structure of Psalms 42 & 43:
>By combining Psalm 43 with the interpretation of Psalm 42 unites a recurring refrain previously established in Psalm 42:
> * (a) Lament (42:2-5)
> * (b) *Refrain* (42:6)
> * (a) Lament (42:7-11)
> * (b) *Refrain* (42:12)
> * (a) Prayer (43:1-4)
> * (b) *Refrain* (43:6)

Literary Movements:
> * From a soul that thirsts for God (42:2) to one that praises God (43:4)
> * From being led by memories (42:4) to being led God's light and truth (43:3)
> * From processions at the house of God (42:4) to his alter (43:4)

Main Point:
>When believers turn from memories that plague our past to God who sustains us, we take the first step on a path that leads from a soul in despair to one with exceeding joy.

BODY:
Sub-Points:
- I. The psalmist's memories of the past lead him into despair (42:1-5).
  - A) The psalmist's overwhelming desire is to get to the temple.
  - B) He remembers a time of participation in worship, but for some unknown reason, is no longer able to do so.
    - i. Verses one and two speak of a soul longing for God using the simile of a deer that pants for water in a like manner.
    - ii. The Hebrew verb (*ta'arog*) translated "to long for" is a Hebrew imperfect.
    - iii. The imperfect tense is typically used to express an incomplete action, but is also is used to denote a habitual action.
    - iv. The idea being expressed is that just as a thirsty deer habitually longs for water, so the psalmist's thirsty soul habitually longs for God.
- II. The psalmist moves from worldly references to heavenly references (42:6).
  - A) A spiritually mature believer does not focus on worldly problems because those problems can bring a soul into despair.
    - i. Like an internal memo in the business world that contains a "from" and "to" reference, the same shift is made in the passage from where the psalmist's thoughts originally began to where they end.

    From:
    - * The land of the Jordan (42:6)
    - * The peaks of Hermon (42:6)
    - * Mount Mizar (42:6)

    To:
    - * Your holy hill (43:3)
    - * Your dwelling places (43:3)
    - * The alter of God (43:3)
    - ii. These literary movements reflect a shift in the psalmist's thoughts as he moves from himself and thinking of the problems that plague him to thinking of God and the solution.

III. The psalmist moves from despair to restoration (43:5).
   A) The psalmist noted repeatedly his antagonists (42:9, 43:1) and their repeated bombardment of hurtful questioning.
      i. Have you ever been depressed with circumstances in life and began to think about people who had made you angry?
      ii. Maybe you were hurt by their comments that infuriated you, and this seemed to compound the problem as it moved from bad to worse.
      iii. Over time, we come to see these people as our enemies who contributed to our demise.
      iv. The psalmist is using this rhetoric to make an important point.
      v. The psalmist is not trivializing problems in life and simply telling us to have positive thoughts; he emphasizes the hurtful force expressed in derogatory statements and encourages the reader to focus on the one who can solve these problems.

SUMMATION:

By applying the psalmist's principles expressed in these two psalms, we can instruct the believer to shift his/her focus from worldly problems to Godly solutions. In doing so, we can encourage our homebound church members by reminding them that "the good old days" are not behind us but in front of us.

Final Thoughts:

Noting the literary devices is crucial for proper interpretation of these two psalms. Both of these psalms should be interpreted together, since Psalm 43 provides a fitting conclusion to Psalm 42. By teaching our congregations about the literary devices within these two psalms, the pastor moves the congregation from interpretation to application.

---

[i] Fee and Stuart, *How to Read the Bible*, 137.

[ii] Cuddon, *Dictionary*, 868.

[iii] Stevenson, Angus, Christine A Lindberg, Ed. *New Oxford American Dictionary*, Third Edition (New York: Oxford University Press, 2010), 1728.

[iv] Longman and Dillard, *Introduction*, 253.

[v] Craigie, and Tate, *Psalms*, 325.

[vi] Ibid.

[vii] John Goldingay, *Psalms*: vol. 2, 42-89 (Grand Rapids: Baker Academic Publishing, 2007), 21

[viii] Brown, *Seeing the Psalms*, 149.

[ix] Ibid., 134.

[x] Ibid.

[xi] Pratico and Van Pelt, *Basics*, 166.

[xii] Craigie and Tate, *Psalms*, 329.

[xiii] Brown, *Seeing the Psalms*, 150.

David W. Brown

Chapter 18

Psalm 115
Commentary and Interpretation

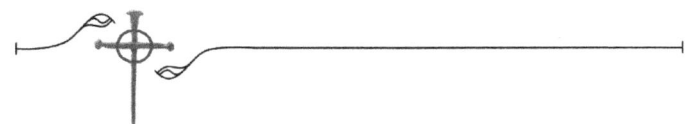

Great sermons teach believers to place their trust in God. As the maker of man, he molds and shapes believers in accordance to his sanctifying will. He smoothes out our rough edges and polishes his people until we are molded and shaped into his image. By contrast, those who spend their lives focusing on idols become molded and shaped into the image of those idols.

Psalm 115 is part of a larger grouping of psalms (110-118) that all begin or end with the word "Hallelujah."[i] Old Testament scholars generally hold that the psalms were arranged to mirror the history of Israel, from David until after the time of exile.[ii] This psalm in particular is considered to be a psalm of trust, and there are several literary features that characterize psalms of trust. According to Bullock, there are five characteristic features of a psalm of trust that Psalm 115 conveys:

* A Declaration of Trust (115:1)
* An Invitation to Trust (115:10)
* A Basis for Trust (115:12-13)
* A Petition (115:14-15)
* A Vow to Praise (115:17)[iii]

However, Bullock warned that somewhere in the shadows of the psalms of trust, trouble lurked that forced the psalmist into declaring his trust for God.[iv] He also commented that the spirit of trusting is directly proportional to the intensity of distress or depth of trouble.[v] Psalms of trust teach believers to place our trust in God, who is metaphorically described in this psalm as the believer's shield.

The trouble in this psalm emerges in the form of contrasting trusts (*betach*) and where to place them. Over and over, the psalmist emphasizes that our trust should be with God in Heaven rather than with the idols of the world. These characteristic features of contrasting trusts build to a theological climax that emphasizes that we become like the things we worship.[vi] This theme is mentioned throughout the Bible and is clearly recognizable in Jeremiah 2:5 where the author declares, "This is what the Lord says: what fault did your fathers find in me, that they strayed so far from me? They chased after worthless idols and became worthless themselves." Israel's slide into idolatry became a situation of national demoralization.[vii]

The theme of becoming like the things we focus on in life is crucial for proper interpretation of this psalm. In Psalm 115, this theme serves to emphasize the contrast of being molded and shaped into the image of God or molded and shaped into the image of the world. Historically speaking, apostate Israel's fascination with idols led them to take on all of the characteristics of the idols they had become so enamored with. They had eyes and ears as well, but like their idols, they could not see God working in their lives, nor could they hear him. The psalmist is emphasizing the notion that from a spiritual perspective, Israel was dead.[viii] This theme and its characteristic features can be seen below in the following outline:

> * Their idols are silver and gold, (115:4)
> The work of man's hands.
> They have mouths, but they cannot speak; (115:5)
> They have eyes, but they cannot see;
> They have ears, but they cannot hear; (1115:6)
> They have noses, but they cannot smell;
> They have hands, but they cannot feel; (115:7)
> They have feet, but they cannot walk;
> They cannot make a sound with their throats.
> Those who make them will become like them, (115:8)
> Everyone who trusts in them.

As G.K. Beale pointed out, "the conclusion about those who make and worship idols is one of the most explicit keys to understanding the nature of idolatry and what happens to people who commit themselves to worshiping and loving their idols: 'Those who make [the idols] will become like [the idols], everyone who trusts in them' (115:8)."[ix] In the postexilic world of Judaism, passages that dealt with idolatry would have been a lasting reminder of the deep scar carved into the collective memory of Israel who had foolishly abandoned their God for idols.[x] In doing so, Israel became dead and lifeless, just like the idols they had worshiped. The main point of Psalm 115 is that believers are called to put their trust in God, who is in Heaven, rather than in worldly possessions (which are idols) that turn the believer's heart into the same, a lifeless object. The first three verses of this psalm begin with a community plea for Israel to turn their hearts to God.

The first sub-point is the psalmist teaches that we become like the things we spend our lives focusing on, and this sub-point is supported by verses four through eight. Notice all of the sensory devices of the idols are mentioned in these verses, but none of them work, and this reflects a contrast from dead idols to a living God. The Hebrew particle "not" (*lo*) is repeated seven times from verse five through seven. The significance of these seven negations reflects the contrast that God has body parts that work, while those of the idols can do nothing. The inability of the idols to speak, see, hear, smell, touch, and walk reflects the limitations of their gods and are contrasted by a living God in Heaven who has boundless freedom.[xi] J.P. Fokkelman claimed that each time one of these seven negations lashed out at them, one of their faculties was destroyed.[xii] When an individual has lost all sensory perception and has no locomotion, they are considered dead.

As a pastor, one of the most challenging tasks in the church is to turn the believers' attention to God and away from worldly possessions. The problem of idolatry is ever-present in the modern world. We may not carve the idols ourselves, but there are plenty of them in today's world, and we foolishly bow down to them by spending the majority of our lives pursuing the idols of money, fame, and worldly success.

The second sub-point is the psalmist encourages Israel to put their trust in God. This sub-point is supported by verses nine through eleven.

There is a clear contrast reflected by the repeated use of the verb "trust" (*batach*). Over and over again, the psalmist teaches believers to "trust in Yahweh" (*betach ba Yahweh*) as opposed to those who had placed their trust in idols in verse eight. As mentioned previously, repeated words or phrases place an emphasis on the context, and Israel is told three times in verses nine through eleven where to place their trust. Goldingay claimed the repeated emphasis to trust in God refers to three groups: the nation, the priests, and the people.[xiii] All three groups are challenged to place their trust in God,[xiv] and this emphasis clearly applies to believers in modern times.

In addition, the psalmist also repeatedly tells Israel that God is their "help and their shield (115:9-11)." Israel's catastrophic failure to place their trust in God could not be more obvious from their history. If their idols, in whom the Jews had placed their trust in, were so powerful, why did their idols fail to deliver them from the Babylonians? The answer is that God is our protector, not idols.

The third sub-point is the psalmist assures Israel of God's blessings, and this is supported by verses twelve through fourteen. Another repeated word in verses twelve and thirteen is the word for "bless" (*vrkh*). The Hebrew verb is used in the imperfect that can denote a habitual action.[xv] Set in a context where the verb is used repeatedly, the psalmist is clearly emphasizing that God will bless them habitually, and verse fourteen explains how. Yahweh will add to them. He will multiply their offspring. Worthless idols in Israel's history did not bless anyone, nor do they bless us in modern times. While some may argue that God blesses believers by giving them money, there are countless examples of those who have enormous amounts of money, yet their lives are disasters. America needs to open its eyes and turn to our Lord Jesus, who can, and will, bless us in ways that will fulfill our souls.

However, the Lord will not bless those who fail to sing his praises. Allen makes this specific point in his commentary on 1 Corinthians 12:2-3. Paul addressed gentiles who once "were led astray to idols that could not speak" but now belonged to the church, in which the proclamation that Jesus was Lord and was heard on the lips of his worshippers.[xvi] This contrasted condition of the heart emphasizes the difference between those who placed their trust in idols and those who placed their trust in God.

The psalmist, however, continues on to teach of a radical transformation that will take place in the life of the worshipper. Those who place their trust in God will be transformed into his image, but those whose trust focuses on the idols of the world will be transformed into their image, so those focused on money will become greedy, and those focused on immorality will become immoral. Former astronaut and senator, John Glenn used the same concept when he said, "A life spent centering only on itself will in the end occupy a very, very small universe."[xvii] We become like the things we focus on in life. What will become of you?

David W. Brown

Trusting God to Shape Believers into His Divine Image:
A Psalm of Trust
Psalm 115

INTRODUCTION:
Structure:
There are five characteristic features of a psalm of trust that Psalm 115 conveys:
* A Declaration of Trust (115:1)
* An Invitation to Trust (115:10)
* A Basis for Trust (115:12-13)
* A Petition (115:14-15)
* A Vow to Praise (115:17)

Somewhere in the shadows of the psalms of trust, trouble lurked that forced the psalmist into declaring his trust for God. Also, the spirit of trusting is directly proportional to the intensity of distress or depth of trouble.

Theological Theme:
We become like the things we worship.

Examples of this theme:
Jeremiah 2:5
This is what the Lord says: what fault did your fathers find in me, that they strayed so far from me? They chased after worthless idols and became worthless themselves.

Psalm 115:4-8
Their idols are silver and gold, (115:4)
The work of man's hands.
They have mouths, but they cannot speak; (115:5)
They have eyes, but they cannot see;
They have ears, but they cannot hear; (115:6)
They have noses, but they cannot smell;

They have hands, but they cannot feel; (115:7)
They have feet, but they cannot walk;
They cannot make a sound with their throats.
Those who make them will become like them, (115:8)
Everyone who trusts in them.

Main Point:
Believers are called to put their trust in God who is in Heaven rather than in worldly possessions (idols) that turn the believer's heart into the same, lifeless objects.

BODY:
Sub-Points
  I. **The psalmist teaches that we become like the things we spend our lives focusing on (115:4-8).**
  A) All of the sensory devices of the idols are mentioned in these verses, but none of them work, and this reflects a contrast from dead idols to a living God.
  i. The Hebrew particle "not" (*lo*) is repeated seven times from verse five through seven.
  ii. The significance of these seven negations reflects the contrast that God has body parts that work while those of the idols can do nothing.
  iii. The inability of the idols to speak, see, hear, smell, touch, and walk reflects the limitations of idols and are contrasted by a living God in heaven who has unbounded freedom.
  iv. J.P. Fokkelman claimed that each time one of these seven negations lashed out at them, one of their faculties was destroyed.
  v. When an individual has lost all sensory perception and has no locomotion, they are considered dead.
  B) One of the most challenging tasks in the church is to turn the believers' attention to God and away from worldly possessions (modern day idols).

II. The psalmist encourages Israel to put their trust in God (115:9-11).
  A) There is a clear contrast reflected by the repeated use of the verb "trust" (*batach*).
    i. Over and over again, the psalmist teaches believers to "trust in Yahweh" (*betach ba Yahweh*), as opposed to those who had placed their trust in idols in verse eight.
    ii. As mentioned previously, repeated words or phrases place an emphasis on the context, and Israel is told three times in verses nine through eleven where to place their trust.
    iii. Goldingay claimed the repeated emphasis to trust in God refers to three groups: the nation, the priests, and the people. All three groups are challenged to place their trust in God, and this emphasis clearly applies to believers in modern times.
III. The psalmist assures Israel of God's blessings (115:12-14).
  A) Another repeated word in verses twelve and thirteen is the word for "bless" (*vrkh*). The Hebrew verb is used in the imperfect that can denote a habitual action.
    i. Set in a context where the verb is used repeatedly, the psalmist is clearly emphasizing that God will bless them habitually, and verse fourteen explains how. Yahweh will add to them. He will multiply their offspring.
    ii. Worthless idols in Israel's history did not bless anyone, nor do they bless us in modern times.
    iii. Some may argue that God blesses believers by giving us money, though there are countless examples of those who have enormous amounts of money, yet their lives are disasters.
  B) America needs to open its eyes and turn to our Lord Jesus, who can bless them in many ways.

SUMMATION:

Believers are called to put their trust in God who is in Heaven, rather than in worldly possessions that turn the believer's heart into the same lifeless objects idols are. In this psalm, the author emphasizes an important theological ideal to them; namely that we become like the things we worship.

GROUNDED: Anchoring the Evangelical Sermon in Theological Doctrine

In 1 Corinthians 12:2-3, Paul addressed gentiles who once "were led astray to idols that could not speak" but now belonged to the church in which the proclamation that Jesus was Lord was heard on the lips of the worshippers. This contrasted condition of the heart emphasizes the difference between those who place their trust in idols and those who place their trust in God.

Final Thoughts:

The significance of recognizing the theological theme in Psalm 115 is crucial for interpretation, since it reflects the outcome of where we have placed our attention and trust in life. The psalmist repeatedly encourages believers to place their trust in God rather than the idols of the world.

---

[i] Fee and Stuart, *How to Read the Bible*, 142. In Psalm 115 the word "Hallelujah" appears at the end of the psalm.

[ii] Ibid., 132.

[iii] Bullock, *Encountering*, 169.

[iv] Ibid. 166.

[v] Ibid.

[vi] G. K. Beale, *We Become What We Worship: A Biblical Theology of Idolatry* (Downers Grove: IVP Academic Publishing, 2008.), 16. See also Bullock, Encountering, 175.

[vii] Leslie C. Allen, *Word Biblical Commentary*, Psalms 101-150 (Nashville: Thomas Nelson Publishing, 2002), 146.

[viii] Fee and Stuart, *How To Read the Bible*, 202. The theological notion that Israel was spiritually dead can be seen in Ezekiel's vision of the valley of dry bones (Ezekiel 37:3) where the question is asked, "Son of Man, can these bones live?" In order for this to happen there must be a resurrection of the people brought about by Yahweh and his spirit.

[ix] Beale, *We Become What We Worship*, 142.

[x] Larry R. Helyer, *Exploring Jewish Literature of the Second Temple Period: A Guide for New Testament Students* (Downers Grove: InterVarsity Press, 2002), 18-19.

[xi] Brown, *Seeing the Psalms*, 172.

[xii] J.P. Fokkelman, *Major Poems of the Hebrew Bible*. Vol. 2-3 (Boston: Brill Academic Publishing,2002-3), 3:225.

[xiii] Goldingay, *Psalms*, 3:332.

[xiv] Ibid.

[xv] Pratico and Van Pelt, *Basics*, 166.

[xvi] Allen, *Psalms*, 3:150

[xvii] Dole, *Hearts*, 122.

Sermons about the Temple and Worship

David W. Brown

Chapter 19

Ezekiel 43:1 - 9
Commentary and Interpretation

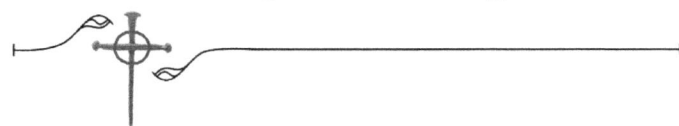

Great sermons emphasize the fulfillment of Old Testament prophesies in the person and work of Jesus Christ. Jesus' sacrificial death on the cross is widely understood as the perfect sacrifice that replaced the animal sacrificial system practiced in Old Testament Judaism. In a similar fashion, Jesus' body is viewed as typological fulfillment and as the replacement of the temple as well.

Paul Hoskins rightly pointed out that the tabernacle was the antecedent to the temple and was constructed as a sanctuary by the people so that the Lord might dwell among them.[i] There are at least five Old Testament passages that point to the limitations of the Jerusalem Temple and its replacement.[ii] In every case, God's glory is portrayed as departing a temporary location to a new location that better reflects his greatness. In the first of these passages, 1 Samuel 4:21-22, the surrounding context describes the Philistines' victory over Israel and their capture of the Ark of the Covenant. The capturing of the ark by the Philistines is portrayed in verse twenty-two as the symbolic departing of God's glory from Israel. In fact, Eli's daughter-in-law gave birth to her son and named the child Ichabod, which means "the glory has departed."[iii] As a result, the glory of God is symbolically portrayed as leaving Israel. This symbolic departure of God's glory in 1 Samuel builds to a theological climax and foreshadows the literal departure of God's glory in the temple by the time of Ezekiel.

The second passage, Psalm 78:60, chronicles the battle between the Philistines and Israel that resulted in the Philistines' victory and the capture of the ark. Shiloh was the early site of God's dwelling place in Canaan where Joshua established the "tent of meeting." Therefore, it is not a coincidence that in the Septuagint (LXX), the word for tent (*skenoma*) comes from the Greek (*skenoo*) that is typically translated as "tabernacle" or "temple."[iv] Verse sixty records God's abandonment of Shiloh as God's dwelling place with man.

Jeremiah 7:12-14, the third passage, also narrates God's displeasure with Israel's idolatry by abandoning his house (the temple). In particular, Jeremiah 7:14 reflects God's willful departure of his house, just as he had abandoned his tent at Shiloh. The fourth and fifth passages that point to the limitations of the Jerusalem temple and its replacement are found in Ezekiel 10:18-19 and 11:22-23. These passages describe God's glory departing the temple and then standing over a mountain east of the city of Jerusalem.

The compounding effect of all five of these passages reflects God's temporary dwelling in these temples and his departure from them. A new, eternal temple is mentioned in this passage, and this is a major part of the prophetic hope for the future of Israel as recorded in both Jeremiah and Ezekiel. This backdrop is crucial for proper interpretation because this passage is part of a larger context (Ezekiel 40-48) that deals with the restoration of God's presence among his people.[v] Lamar Cooper emphasized this point in his commentary when he wrote:

> As a part of the restoration, God promised that he would again be the Shepherd of Israel and that he would dwell with them in a unique way (Ezek. 34:30). The temple of Ezekiel's vision made that promise a reality by looking to a future day when God would personally dwell again with his people (Rev. 7:15-17; 21:3-4).[vi]

This leads to the main point: God has only one goal in this passage, and that is to reestablish his presence in this future temple so that he might dwell among his people forever. Daniel Block rightly asserted this point when he wrote:

> The message of "the house" should have been music to the exiles' ears, for it embodied all their hopes and aspirations. Having witnessed the destruction of the temple in 586, and having lived for two decades hundreds of miles away from the sacred site, they must have wondered what had become of Yahweh's ancient promise to dwell among his people.[vii]

The first sub-point in this passage is God's glorious presence will return to dwell among his people, and this is supported by verses one through five. Iain Duguid pointed out that an empty temple is, by itself, worthless.[viii] Temples were made to be occupied, and the significance of the passage is God's restored presence among his people.[ix] In verse one, Ezekiel noted that the spirit of God led him to the gate that was facing east. The direction is significant because the last time the prophet had encountered God's glory was when God had departed from the temple and then stood over a mountain east of the city (Ezekiel 11:22-23).[x] God's glory will return by the same direction it had departed, along the east-west spine of the temple, and this has special significance from the standpoint of restoration. Block pointed out the significance of this event was that it indicated the period of separation between God and Israel had come to a close.[xi] The story serves also to heighten the emphasis of God's promise in Hebrews 13:5, where the author alludes to several Old Testament verses that God will never leave or forsake his people. God is a helper to his people, and he will protect them.[xii]

The second sub-point is that God redefines his temple space to ensure his holiness, and this is supported in verses six and seven. Ezekiel's reference in verse seven to the throne as a place for the soles of his feet reflects God's divine initiative to assert kingship over Israel. However, part of God's restoration comes from limiting access to the holy places that Israel had defiled in the past.[xiii] By redefining and limiting access to these sacred places, God asserts his Kingship over Israel to last forever.[xiv] Duguid emphasized this point in his commentary when he wrote:

> In the past, the house of Israel had defiled the Lord's name by their prostitution (i.e., their spiritual adultery

> with the god's of other nations, as in ch. 23) and by setting up memorial stelae to their monarchs within the temple grounds (43:7-8). There is no room for these stelae in honor of the human kings in the place dedicated to the divine king. Henceforth, they will be banished. Indeed the whole former social geography of the temple mount, where the house of the divine King was merely a (smaller) neighboring residence to the palace of the human king, will be swept away. Because the former kings defiled the Lord's name by their detestable practices, their position in the future kingdom will be further removed from the center.[xv]

This practice of redefining and limiting access to these sacred spaces continues into the New Testament as well. In the New Testament, God's sacred space is redefined in an even greater way in the person of Jesus Christ. This point is emphasized in John 2:18-22 where Jesus declares himself to be the new temple and dwelling place of God. However, instead of being a man-made temple that his people enter into and risk defiling, this sacred space becomes the embodiment of God and cannot be defiled.

The third sub-point is God's future dwelling place points to an everlasting temple in which he will dwell with his people, and this is supported by verse nine. In this verse, the Israelites are challenged to remove their spiritual harlotry and pagan funerary practices so that God might dwell with them forever.[xvi] The challenge is issued through the verb "let them put far away" (*yerachaqu*), which appears in the jussive. The jussive conjugation in Hebrew is used to express either some type of mild command or strong wish.[xvii] Since verses seven through nine are framed by verbs dealing with spiritual prostitution or harlotry, the emphasis becomes one of guarding the sacred space of the temple so that God might dwell with his people. Block noted in these verses that nothing with God had changed, and Israel could not carry on as she had prior to Yahweh's departure in 586 B.C.[xviii] The pagan practices that were detestable then continue to be detestable. Therefore, it is Israel who must change.

In today's evangelical pulpits, where prosperity sermons and business models have become common place, Ezekiel reminds believers with chilling clarity that sacred places like the church must be guarded as well. The pulpit is the place to proclaim God's word, not a pedestal to an elite few for the acquisition of wealth. Jesus was not nailed to a cross so believers could get rich. He ransomed his life for believers, and now we are indebted to him. One day, he will return to collect that debt.

David W. Brown

New Temples, Sacred Spaces and the Presence of God: Preparation and Declarations for Worship
Ezekiel 43:1-9

INTRODUCTION:
Theological Theme:
Jesus' sacrificial death on the cross is widely understood as the perfect sacrifice that replaced the animal sacrificial system practiced in Old Testament Judaism. In a similar fashion, Jesus' body is viewed as typological fulfillment as the replacement of the temple.

Temple Limitations:
There are at least five Old Testament passages that point to the limitations of the Jerusalem Temple and its replacement:

1 Samuel 4:21-22: The capturing of the ark by the Philistines is portrayed in verse twenty-two as the symbolic departing of God's glory from Israel. Eli's daughter-in-law gave birth to her son and named the child Ichabod, which means "the glory has departed." As a result, the glory of God is symbolically portrayed as leaving Israel.

Psalm 78:60 chronicles the battle between the Philistines and Israel that resulted in the Philistines victory and the capture of the ark. Shiloh was the early site of God's dwelling place in Canaan where Joshua established the "tent of meeting." Therefore, it is not a coincidence that in the LXX the word for tent (*skenoma*) comes from the Greek (*skenoo*) that is typically translated as "tabernacle" or "temple." Verse sixty records God's abandonment of Shiloh as God's dwelling place with man.

Jeremiah 7:12-14 also narrates God's displeasure with Israel's idolatry by abandoning his house (the temple). In particular, verse fourteen reflects God's willful departure of his house just as he had abandoned his tent at Shiloh.

Ezekiel 10:18-19: These verses describe God's glory departing the temple.

Ezekiel 11:22-23: These verses describe God's glory as standing over a mountain east of the city of Jerusalem then departing Israel.

Compounding Emphasis:

The compounding effect of all five of these passages reflects God's temporary dwelling in these temples and his departure from them.

Main Point:

God has only one goal in this passage, and that is to reestablish his presence in this future temple so that he might dwell among his people forever.

BODY:
Sub-Points:

I. God's glorious presence will return to dwell among his people (43:1-5).
   A) An empty temple is worthless. Temples were made to be occupied, and the significance of the passage is God's restored presence among his people.
   B) In verse one, Ezekiel noted that the spirit of God led him to the gate that was facing east.
      i. The direction is significant because the last time the prophet had encounter God's glory was when God had departed from the temple and then stood over a mountain east of the city (Ezekiel 11:22-23).
      ii. Thus, God's glory returns by the same direction it had departed, along the east-west spine of the temple, and this has special significance from the standpoint of restoration.
      iii. The significance of this event was that it indicated that the period of separation between God and Israel had come to a close.
   C) The story also serves to heighten the emphasis of God's promise in Hebrews 13:5 where the author alludes to several Old Testament verses that he will never leave or forsake his people. God is a helper to his people, and he will protect them.

II. God redefines his temple space to ensure his holiness (43:6-7).
   A) Ezekiel's reference in verse seven to the throne as a place for the soles of his feet reflects God's divine initiative to assert kingship over Israel.
      i. Part of God's restoration comes from limiting access to the holy places that Israel had defiled in the past.
      ii. By redefining and limiting access to these sacred places, God asserts his Kingship over Israel to last forever.
      iii. This practice of redefining and limiting access to these sacred spaces continues into the New Testament as well.
      iv. In the New Testament, God's sacred space is redefined in an even greater way in the person of Jesus Christ.
      v. This point is emphasized in John 2:18-22 where Jesus declares himself to be the new temple and dwelling place of God.
      vi. Instead of being a man-made temple that his people enter into and risk defiling, this sacred space becomes the embodiment of God and cannot be defiled.

III. God's future dwelling place points to an everlasting temple in which he will dwell with his people (43:9).
   A) The Israelites are challenged to remove their spiritual harlotry and pagan funerary practices so that God might dwell with them forever.
      i. The challenge is issued through the verb "let them put far away" (*yerachaqu*) which appears in the jussive.
      ii. The jussive conjugation in Hebrew is used to express either some type of mild command or a strong wish.
      iii. Since verses seven through nine are framed by verbs dealing with spiritual prostitution or harlotry, the emphasis becomes one of guarding the sacred space of the temple so that God might dwell with his people.

SUMMATION:

God's promise to dwell among his people was made a reality by pointing to this future vision. God redefines and limits access to his future temple so as not to allow this future sacred space to be defiled.

Final Thoughts:
This is a passage where typological fulfillment is being presented to the reader. In order to grasp this concept, the pastor must educate his congregation on this type of replacement theology. The notion that Jesus becomes the new temple is profound in both Mark's and John's Gospels.

---

[i] Paul Hoskins, *Jesus as the Fulfillment of the Temple in the Gospel of John* (Waynesboro: Paternoster Press, 2006), 39.

[ii] Ibid., 105. The five passage are 1 Sam. 4:21-22; Psalm 78:60; Jeremiah 7:12-14 Ezekiel 10:18-19, and Ezekiel 11:22-23.

[iii] Judson Cornwall & Stelman Smith, *The Exhaustive Dictionary of Biblical Names: A complete listing of every name in the Bible with its various shades of Greek or Hebrew meaning*, (Atachu: Bridges-Logos Press, 1998), 82.

[iv] Taylor, *Analytical Lexicon to the Septuagint*, 494.

[v] Fee and Stuart, *How to Read the Bible*, 202.

[vi] Lamar Eugene Cooper, Sr. *The New American Commentary: An Exegetical and Theological Exposition of the Holy Scripture NIV Text, Ezekiel* (Nashville: Broadman & Holman Publishing, 1994), 378.

[vii] Daniel I. Block, *The New International Commentary on the Old Testament, The Book of Ezekiel, Chapters 25-48* (Grand Rapids: William B. Eerdmans Publishing, 1998), 588.

[viii] Iain M. Duguid, *The NIV Application Commentary, Ezekiel* (Grand Rapids: Zondervan Publishing, 1999), 489.

[ix] Ibid.

[x] Block, *Ezekiel*, 25-48, 578.

[xi] Duguid, *Ezekiel*, 578-79.

[xii] G.K. Beale and D.A. Carson, *Commentary on the New Testament Use of the Old Testament* (Grand Rapids: Baker Academic Publishing, 2007.), 991-92.

[xiii] Duguid, *Ezekiel*, 489.

[xiv] Ibid.

[xv] Ibid., 489-90.

[xvi] Block, *Ezekiel*, 586.

[xvii] Pratico and Van Pelt, *Basics*, 131.

[xviii] Block, *Ezekiel*, 582.

David W. Brown

Chapter 20

John 4:7 - 26
Commentary and Interpretation

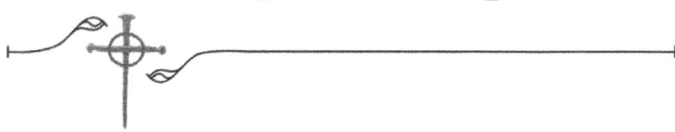

Great sermons emphasize the importance of worship. Worship in spirit and truth does not focus on music or entertainment, but rather focuses the believer on Jesus, because he alone is the new temple in which believers worship him as Lord. If believers are going to worship God, we are called not to come to a particular geographical location, but rather to come to Jesus. This passage in John's Gospel emphasizes this point.

John 4:7-26 is made up of two paragraphs that are tied together by a common phrase. The passage is framed by the phrase "Jesus said to her" (*legei aute o Ieasous.*)[i] The context of this passage, however, is significant because verses twenty through twenty-four are one of the four[ii] locations in John's Gospel where New Testament scholars have identified Jesus as being the replacement for the temple.[iii] To grasp this passage, the pastor must first understand all four locations and the cumulative effect they have.[iv] A summation of these four passages is needed.

The first passage is John 1:14 where the author writes, "The word became flesh and dwelt among us, and we beheld his glory, the glory of an only begotten from the Father, full of grace and truth." The verb "dwelt" (*eskenosen*) comes from *skenoo*, which is typically translated in the Old Testament LXX as "tent" used in the "tent of meeting," which is a common reference to the tabernacle.[v]

John 1:51 is the second passage; the author wrote "And He said to him, truly, truly, I say to you, you shall see the heavens opened, and the angels of God ascending and descending on the Son of Man." John 1:51 is an allusion to Genesis 28:12 that records Jacob's vision at Bethel. The Hebrew term "Bethel" means "house of God."[vi] The significance of John 1:51 is found in the fact that the Son of Man, rather than Bethel, is now the new location where God reveals himself to his people.[vii] Jesus is the new house, or temple, where the presence of God dwells.[viii]

Third, in John 2:18-22, Jesus says to the Jews, "Destroy this temple, and in three days I will raise it up." They think Jesus is talking about the temple building, claiming it took forty-six years to build, but in verse twenty-one, John teaches that Jesus was talking about the temple of his body. There is also a grammatical issue that supports Jesus' body is the true temple. In John 2:19, the antecedent of the personal pronoun "it" (*auton*) is the "temple" (*naon*).[ix] This is important from an interpretational standpoint, since the grammar emphasizes a theology that Jesus is the new temple.

Finally, the issues that lie at the heart of John 4:20-24 are how to worship the Father and the location of the temple. The Samaritans had built their own temple at Mt. Gerizim, but the Jewish ruler John Hyrcanus destroyed this in 129 B.C. Perceiving Jesus to be a prophet, the Samaritan woman opens a discussion on one of the most significant issues that separated the Jews and the Samaritans.[x] For his part, Jesus advocated that worship in spirit and truth made any geographical location obsolete.[xi] Location no longer mattered when it came to worship.[xii] True worship must bridge the gap between such issues. If one wants to worship the Father, they must come to Jesus. He is the new temple in which believers now worship.[xiii]

All four of these passages have a cumulative effect that impacts the interpretation of Jesus' conversation with the Samarian woman at the well. Since the Samaritan woman discusses worship and the location of where to worship, John's Gospel portrays Jesus as the new locus in which the believer is called to worship. In him the presence of God now dwells. By doing so, John advances a theological theme that moves the dwelling place of God from the temple to Jesus. In other words, the theme moves from the temple of God to God as the temple.[xiv] This leads to the main point of the passage and that is true worship of God is not based upon one's geographical location, but rather on the individual coming to Jesus. Jesus is the new temple in which the presence of God dwells.

The first sub-point is true worship must bridge an ethnic gulf, and this is supported in verse nine. The rift between the Jews and Samaritans was thoroughly entrenched through generations of bitterness, and the problem was made even worse in 129 B.C. when Hyrcanus destroyed the Samaritan's Temple on Mt. Gerizim.[xv] John highlights the cultural rift between these two groups through a series of contrasts in the stories of Nicodemus in chapter three and the Samaritan woman at the well in chapter four. The contrasts can be seen below:

Nicodemus	Samaritan Woman
* Came at night	* Came during the day
* Religious Elite (Pharisee)	* Religious outcast
* Jewish Man	* Samaritan woman
* Did not receive Jesus' message (3:11)	* Received Jesus' message

The ethnic barrier that existed between these two groups stood as a lasting reminder of the goal of true worship. Worship in spirit and truth must bridge the gap between people groups, and Jesus' initiation of a conversation with this woman opened the door to closing that gap. Albert Schweitzer once said, "Sometimes our light goes out but is blown into flame by another human being. Each of us owes our deepest thanks to those who have rekindled the light."[xvi] From Schweitzer's perspective, Jesus has rekindled that light with the Samaritan woman by bridging the ethnic gulf.

The second sub-point is that true worship must bridge a moral gulf, and this is supported in verses sixteen through eighteen. In the ancient world, drawing water from a well was a task typically performed in the mornings when the water was cool. The fact that the Samaritan woman comes at noon most likely reflects that her community had ostracized her.[xvii] The story of the Samaritan woman at the well is a classic example of someone jaded by life, yet our loving Lord reaches out to build a relationship with her. In a 1983 article, Laurence Cantwell noted that the woman's life was not so much immoral (though it is that!) as it was a mess that consisted of a series of false beginnings and shattered hopes.[xviii] From this perspective, the woman's life reflects a regular state of broken relationships. She had five failed marriages and now was living with someone who was not her husband. When we add the notion of fetching water at noon in an effort to avoid further ridicule by the community in which she lived, we can begin to envision a woman who had reached rock bottom in life. True worship reaches across these moral gulfs, where people have become objects of ridicule, to find an individual worn down by life. If there was anyone who needed the Lord, it was this woman. True worship in the new temple crosses these moral gulfs and grants access to those that life has swept aside.

The third sub-point is that true worship must bridge a religious gulf, and this supported by verses twenty and twenty-one. The Samaritans held to their own version of the Pentateuch, and this severely truncated their knowledge of God by restricting their canon of Scripture to the first five books of the Old Testament.[xix] As a result, the Samaritan's began to search the Scriptures where God had commanded their forefathers to seek a place where the Lord would put his name (Deut. 12:5).[xx] The Samaritans believed this place to be Mt. Gerizim, but the Pharisees, who held to the entire Old Testament, believed this place to be Jerusalem.

The disagreement over their canon of Scripture and the location of where to worship was an obvious stumbling block between the two groups. By rendering both locations as obsolete, Jesus bridges the gap by becoming the new location of worship. In addition, worship in the new temple changed the dynamic from past worship done by "their fathers" (*panters*) to present worship of "the Father" (*patri*).[xxi] In doing so, Jesus reached across the religious barriers that separated the Jews and Samaritans for centuries. By becoming the new temple, Jesus bridged the ethnic, moral, and religious barriers that prevented believers from building a stronger relationship with our Lord.

Temples, Worship, and Outcasts:
Moving from the Temple of God to God as the Temple
John 4:7-26

INTRODUCTION:

Structure:

The passage is made up of two paragraphs that are tied together by a common phrase. The entire passage is framed by the phrase "Jesus said to her" (*legei aute o Ieasous*).

Typological Replacement:

There are four passages in John's Gospel that describe Jesus as the replacement for the temple:

- John 1:14—"dwelt" (*eskenosen*) is from *skenoo*, which is typically translated in the Old Testament LXX as "tent" used in the "tent of meeting," which is a common reference to the tabernacle.
- John 1:51—John 1:51 is an allusion to Genesis 28:12 that records Jacob's vision at Bethel. The Hebrew term translated as "Bethel" means "house of God." The significance of John 1:51 is found in the fact that the Son of Man, rather than Bethel, is now the new location where God reveals himself to his people.
- John 2:18-22—In this passage, Jesus says to the Jews, "Destroy this temple, and in three days I will raise it up." They think Jesus is talking about the temple building, claiming it took forty-six years to build, but in verse twenty-one, John teaches that Jesus was talking about the temple of his body.
- John 4:20-24—The issues that lie at the heart of John 4:20-24 are how to worship the Father and the location of the temple. The Samaritans had built their own temple at Mt. Gerizim, but John Hyrcanus destroyed this in 129 BC. Perceiving Jesus to be a prophet, the Samaritan woman opens a discussion on one of the most significant issues that separated the Jews and the Samaritans. For his part, Jesus advocated that worship in spirit and truth made any geographical location obsolete.

Theological Theme:
　　John advances a theological theme that moves the dwelling place of God from the temple to Jesus. The theme moves from the temple of God to God as the temple.

Main Point:
　　True worship of God is not based upon one's geographical location, but on the individual coming to Jesus, who is the new temple in which the presence of God dwells.

BODY:
Sub-Points:
　　I. **True worship must bridge an ethnic gulf (4:9).**
　　　A) The rift between the Jews and Samaritans was thoroughly entrenched through generations of bitterness, and the problem was made even worse in 129 BC when John Hyrcanus destroyed the Samaritan's Temple on Mt. Gerizim.
　　　　i. John highlights the rift between these two groups through a series of contrasts in the stories of Nicodemus in chapter three and the Samaritan woman at the well in chapter four.

Nicodemus	Samaritan Woman
* Came at night	* Came during the day
* Religious Elite (Pharisee)	* Religious outcast
* Jewish Man	* Samaritan woman
* Did not receive Jesus' message (3:11)	* Received Jesus' message

　　　B) Albert Schweitzer once said, "Sometimes our light goes out but is blown into flame by another human being. Each of us owes our deepest thanks to those who have rekindled the light."
　　　　i. From Schweitzer's perspective, Jesus has rekindled that light with the Samaritan woman by bridging the ethnic gulf.
　　II. **True worship must bridge a moral gulf (4:16-18).**
　　　A) In the ancient world, drawing water from a well was a task typically performed in the mornings when the water was cool. The fact that the Samaritan woman comes at noon most likely reflects that her community had ostracized her.

    i. Laurence Cantwell noted that the woman's life was not so much immoral (though it is that!) as it was a mess that consisted of a series of false beginnings and shattered hopes.
    ii. From this perspective, the woman's life reflected a regular state of broken relationships. She had five failed marriages, and now was living with someone who was not her husband. When we add the notion of fetching water at noon in an effort to avoid further ridicule by the community in which she lived, we can begin to envision a woman who had reached rock bottom in life.
    iii. True worship reaches across these moral gulfs where people have become objects of ridicule to find an individual worn down by life. If there was anyone who needed the Lord, it was this woman. True worship in the new temple crosses these moral gulfs and grants access to those that life has swept aside.
III. True worship must bridge a religious gulf (4:20-21).
 A) The Samaritans held to their own version of the Pentateuch, and this severely truncated their knowledge of God by restricting their canon of Scripture to the first five books of the Old Testament.
  i. As a result, the Samaritans began to search the Scriptures where God had commanded their forefathers to seek a place where the Lord would put his name (Deut.12:5).
  ii. The Samaritans believed this place to be Mt. Gerizim, but the Jews, who held to the entire Old Testament, believed this place to be Jerusalem.
  iii. The disagreement over their canon of Scripture and the location of where to worship was a stumbling block between the two groups.

SUMMATION:
  This is a passage that teaches believers that true worship of God is not based upon one's geographical location, but rather on the individual coming to Jesus, who is the new temple in which the presence of God dwells.

By becoming the new temple, Jesus bridged the ethnic, moral, and religious barriers that prevented believers from building a stronger relationship with our Lord.

Final Thoughts:
If the congregation is going to grasp this passage, they must first be taught about typological replacement theology and its fulfillment. This could easily be accomplished through a series of studies on typological fulfillment with this sermon as a climax.

---

[i] The passage begins (4:7) and ends (4:26) with the phrase "Jesus said to her." The phrase is used in 4:1, 17, 21, and 26.

[ii] The four passages in John's Gospel that describe Jesus as the replacement for the temple are 1:14, 1:51, 2:18-22, and 4:20-24.

[iii] Hoskins, *Jesus as the Fulfillment*, 108-46.

[iv] I would highly recommend reading both of Paul Hoskins books, *Jesus as the Fulfillment of the Temple in the Gospel of John* (Waynesboro: Paternoster Press, 2006) and *That Scripture Might be Fulfilled: A Typology and the Death of Christ* (Maitland: Xulon Press, 2009). Both of these texts discuss the subject of typological fulfillment in depth.

[v] Hoskins, *Fulfillment*, 117.

[vi] Judson Cornwall & Stelman Smith, *Dictionary of Biblical Names*, 31.

[vii] David A. deSilva, *Honor, Patronage, Kinship & Purity: Unlocking New Testament Culture* (Downers Grove: Intervarsity Press, 2000), 292.

[viii] David A. deSilva, *An Introduction to the New Testament: Contexts, Methods & Ministry Formation* (Downers Grove: Intervarsity Press, 2004.), 421.

[ix] Hoskins, *Fulfillment*, 114. Hoskins goes on to site more examples in his book, but due to limitations in this text I only use one.

[x] D.A. Carson, *The Pillar New Testament Commentary, The Gospel According to John* (Grand Rapids: William B. Eerdmans Publishing, 1991), 221-22.

[xi] William A. Simmons, *Peoples of the New Testament World: An Illustrated Guide* (Peabody: Hendrickson Publishers, 2008), 130.

[xii] Andreas J. Köstenburger, *Baker Exegetical Commentary on the New Testament, John* (Grand Rapids: Baker Academic Publishing, 2004), 155.

[xiii] Ibid, 136-37.

[xiv] Andrea Spatafora, *From the Temple of God to God as the Temple: A Biblical Theological Study of the Temple in the Book of Revelation* (Rome: Gregorian University Press, 1997), 101-116. Chapter III discusses Jesus as the replacement for the Temple in the New Testament while pages 101-116 focus particularly on this theme in John's Gospel.

[xv] DeSilva, *Introduction*, 89.

[xvi] Dole, *Hearts*, 84.

[xvii] Bruce J. Malina and Richard Rohrbaugh, *Social-Science Commentary on the Gospel of John* (Minneapolis: Fortress Press Publishing, 1998), 98.

[xviii] Laurence Cantwell, "Immortal Longing in Sermone Humili: A Study of John 4:5-26." in the *Scottish Journal of Theology*, vol. 36. Issue 01, 1983, p. 73-86.

[xix] Köstenburger, *John*, 155-56.

[xx] Carson, *John*, 222.

[xxi] Leon Morris, *The New International Commentary on the New Testament, The Gospel According to John, Revised Edition* (Grand Rapids: William B. Eerdmans Publishing, 1995), 238.

David W. Brown

CONCLUSION

Great sermons come about by performing solid exegesis of a passage so that congregations can grasp the meaning of a biblical story and apply it to their lives. Meaning is found in the context of a passage, and each of these twenty passages tells a story. Like all stories, each one of these has a designated beginning and ending point that are identified by literary devices built into the Scripture. Repeated words not only place an emphasis in the passage, but are oftentimes used to mark the starting and stopping points of the story. These grammatical and literary features should be used to guide pastors and teachers in building sermons and teaching outlines. While chapter divisions and verse numbers are useful in locating the stories, they often hinder interpretation and sermon preparation by setting false boundaries for a given passage.

All biblical passages are stories grounded in the theological doctrines of the Christian faith. The apostles and the reformers of Christian history were people who shaped the lives of believers by grounding them in the immoveable stories of doctrine that anchored their faith. Amidst enormous persecution and, often, the threat of death, they taught and trained Christian believers to persevere in their faith at all costs. This goal has not changed; Christians today need to be grounded in faith, just as they were then.

Knowledge in the areas of Christian history, social setting, biblical language, and theology are all necessary for educating the saints, and they also compliment sermons and teaching outlines by transforming them into literary masterpieces that congregants will remember and apply to their lives. Also, interpretation rooted in history and grounded in grammar prevents the notion that every interpretation is equally valid. Pastors and teachers must begin emphasizing proper interpretation from the pulpit and in their Sunday school classrooms.

Preachers will never aid spiritual growth with dumbed-down sermons. Congregations need and, in my experience as a pastor, are thirsting for someone to teach them God's Word in great detail. Training the hearts and minds of Christian believers is hard work and takes years of commitment, but the end result is a believer who understands the significance of these principle doctrines and teaches others as he/she goes through life.

Since only a small minority of evangelical Christians will ever attend Bible College or seminary, the training must begin in the pulpits and Sunday school classrooms with sermons and teaching outlines that are anchored in theological doctrine. My hopes and prayers are that *Grounded: Anchoring the Evangelical Sermon in Theological Doctrine* has been beneficial to you, as pastors and Sunday school teachers alike, who ground believers in the doctrines of God throughout your own fruit-bearing ministries.

GROUNDED: *Anchoring the Evangelical Sermon in Theological Doctrine*

David W. Brown

BIBLIOGRAPHY

Books

Aland, Barbara, Kurt Aland, Johannes Karavdopoulos, Carlo M. Martini, and Bruce Metzger, eds. *The Greek New Testament*. 4th rev. ed. Stuttgart: Deutsche Bibelgesellschaft, United Bible Societies, 1994.

_____. eds. *Novum Testamentum Graece*, 27th ed. Stuttgart: Deutsche Bibelgesellschaft, 1993.

Allen, Leslie C. *Word Biblical Commentary, Psalms 101-150*. Nashville: Thomas Nelson Publishing. 2002.

Barton, Stephen C. "Parables on God's Love and Forgiveness" in *the Challenge of Jesus' Parables* ed. by Richard N. Longenecker. Grand Rapids: William B. Eerdmans Publishing. 2000.

Bailey, Kenneth E. *Jacob & the Prodigal: How Jesus Retold Israel's Story*. Downers Grove: Intervarsity Press. 2003.

_____. *Poet and the Peasant: A Literary-Cultural Approach to the Parables in Luke*. Grand Rapids: William B. Eerdmans Publishing. 1976.

Bauer, W. Danker, F. W. Arndt, W.F. Gingrich, F.W. *Greek-English Lexicon of the New Testament and Other Early Christian Literature*. Chicago: University of Chicago Press. 2000.

Beale, G.K. *We Become What We Worship: A Biblical Theology of Idolatry*. Downers Grove: IVP Academic Publishing, 2008.

Beale, G.K. and D.A. Carson. *Commentary on the New Testament Use of the Old Testament* Grand Rapids: Baker Academic Publishing. 2007.

Bell, Rob. *Love Wins: A Book Heaven, Hell, And The Fate of Every Person Who Ever Lived*. New York: Harper Collins Publishers. 2011.

Block, Daniel I. *The New International Commentary on the Old Testament, The Book of Ezekiel*. Grand Rapids: William B. Eerdmans Publishing. 1998.

Blomberg, Craig L. *Commentary on the New Testament Use of the Old Testament*: ed. G. K. Beal and D. A. Carson. Grand Rapids: Baker Academic Publishing. 2007.

BIBLIOGRAPHY

_____. *Interpreting the Parables*. Downers Grove: InterVarsity Press. 1990.

_____. *The New American Commentary: Matthew*. Nashville: Broadman Press. 1992.

Blomberg, Craig L. Kamell, Mariam J. *Exegetical Commentary on the New Testament, James*. Grand Rapids: Zondervan Publishing. 2008.

Brake, Donald L. *A Visual History of the English Bible: The Tumultuous Tale of the World's Bestselling Book*. Grand Rapids: Baker Books Publishing. 2008.

Braude, William G. *The Midrash on Psalms:* Yale Judaica Series, Vol. 13. New Haven: Yale University Press, 1959.

Brown, William P. *Seeing the Psalms: A Theology of Metaphor*. Louisville: Westminster John Knox Press. 2002.

Bruner, F.D. *The Christbook*. Waco: Word Publishing. 1987.

Bullock, C. Hassell. *Encountering the Book of Psalms: A Literary and Theological Introduction*. Grand Rapids: Baker Academic Publishing. 2001.

Burge, Gary. Cohick, Lynn. Green, Gene L. *The New Testament in Antiquity: A Survey of the New Testament within its Cultural Contexts*. Grand Rapids: Zondervan Publishing. 2009.

Caragounis, Chrys C. *The Development of Greek and the New Testament: Morphology, Syntax, Phonology, and Textual Transmission*. Grand Rapids: Baker Academic Publishing. 2006.

Carson, D.A. *The Pillar New Testament Commentary, The Gospel According to John*. Grand Rapids: William B. Eerdmans Publishing. 1991.

Carter, Terry G. Duvall, J. Scott. Hays, Daniel J. *Preaching God's Word: A Hands-On Approach to Preparing, Developing, and Delivering the Sermon*. Grand Rapids: Zondervan Publishing. 2005.

Cory, Loyd. *Quote Unquote*. Wheaton: Victor Books Publishing.1977.

Cornwall, Judson and Stelman Smith. *The Exhaustive Dictionary of Biblical Names: A complete listing of every name in the Bible with various shades of Greek or Hebrew meaning*. Atachu: Bridges-Logos Press. 1998.

Cooper, Lamar Eugene Sr. *The New American Commentary: An Exegetical and Theological Exposition of the Holy Scripture NIV Text, Ezekiel*. Nashville: Broadman & Holman Publishing. 1994.

BIBLIOGRAPHY

Cuddon, J.A. Preston, C.E. *The Dictionary of Literary Terms and Literary Theory*, fourth edition. London: Penguin Publishing. 2000.

Craigie, Peter C. Tate, Marvin E. *Word Biblical Commentary, Psalms 1-50*, second edition. Nashville: Thomas Nelson Publishers. 2004.

Cully, Martin C. Mikeal C. Parson. Joshua J. Stigall. *Luke: A Handbook On The Greek Text*. Waco: Baylor University Press. 2010.

Cymbala, Jim. *Fresh Wind, Fresh Fire*. Grand Rapids: Zondervan Publishing. 1997.

DeSilva, David A. *Honor, Patronage, Kinship & Purity: Unlocking New Testament Culture*. Downers Grove: Intervarsity Press. 2000.

_____. *An Introduction to the New Testament: Context, Methods & Ministry Formation*. Downers Grove: Intervarsity Press. 2004.

Dole, Elizabeth. *Hearts Touched with Fire: My 500 Favorite Inspirational Quotations*. New York: Carroll & Graff Publishers, 2004.

Delitzsch, Franz. *Proverbs, Ecclesiastes, and Song of Solomon*. Grand Rapids: William B. Eerdmans Publishing. 1975.

Duguid, Iain M. *The NIV Application Commentary, Ezkiel, Chapters 25-48*. Grand Rapids: William B. Eerdmans Publishing.1999.

Duvall, J. Scott. Hays, J. Daniel. *Grasping God's Word: A Hands-On Approach to Reading, Interpreting, and Applying the Bible* 2nd ed. Grand Rapids: Zondervan Publishing. 2005.

Fee, Gordon D. *Pauline Christology: An Exegetical-Theological Study*. Peabody: Hendrickson Publishing. 2007.

Fee, Gordon D. Stuart, Douglas. *How to Read the Bible Book by Book: A Guided Tour*. Grand Rapids: Zondervan Publishing. 2002.

Fiztmyer, Joseph A. *The Gospel According to Luke X-XXIV*. Garden City: Double Day Publishing. 1985.

Fokkelman, J.P. Major *Poems of the Hebrew Bible*. Vól. 2-3. Boston: Brill Academic Publishing. 2002-3.

BIBLIOGRAPHY

Frie, Hans W. *The Eclipse of Biblical Narrative: A Study of Eighteenth and Nineteenth Century Hermeneutics*. New Haven: Yale University Press. 1993.

Gamble, Harry Y. *Books and Readers in the Early Church: A History of the Early Christian Texts*. New Haven: Yale University Press. 1995.

Garland, David E. *Exegetical Commentary on the New Testament: Luke*: ed. Clinton E. Arnold. Grand Rapids: Zondervan Publishing. 2011.

Garret, Duane A. *The New American Commentary: An Exegetical and Theological Exposition of the Holy Scripture*: NIV Text, vol. 14. Nashville: Broadman Holman Press. 1993.

Greidanus, Sidney. *The Modern Preacher and the Ancient Text: Interpreting and Preaching Biblical Literature*. Grand Rapids: William B. Eerdmans Publishing. 1988.

_____. *Preaching Christ from Ecclesiastes*. Grand Rapids: William B. Eerdmans Publishing. 2010.

Goldingay, John. *Psalms*. Grand Rapids: Baker Academic Publishing. 2006.

Guelich, Robert A. *Word Biblical Commentary*: Mark 1-8 vol. 34a. Grand Rapids: Thomas Nelson Publishing. 1989.

Guthrie, G. H. *The Structure of Hebrews: A Text-Linguistic Analysis*. Grand Rapids: Baker Books Publishing. 1994.

Hagner, Donald A. *Encountering the Book of Hebrews*. Grand Rapids: Baker Academic Publishing. 2002.

_____. *Word Biblical Commentary: Matthew*. Dallas: Word Book Publishing. 1995.

Helyer, Larry R. *Exploring Jewish Literature of the Second Temple Period: A Guide for New Testament Students*. Downers Grove: InverVarsity Press. 2002.

Holgate, David A. *Prodigality, Liberality and Meanness: The Prodigal Son in the Greco-Roman Perspective*. Sheffield: Sheffield Press. 1999.

Hoskins, Paul. *Jesus as the Fulfillment of the Temple in the Gospel of John*. Waynesboro: Paternoster Press. 2006.

_____. *That Scripture Might Be Fulfilled: A Typology and the Death of Christ*. Maitland: Xulon Press. 2009.

BIBLIOGRAPHY

Iverson, Kelly R. *Mark as Story: Retrospect and Prospect*. Atlanta: 2011.

Johnson, Luke Timothy. *The Writings of the New Testament*: 3rd ed. Minneapolis: Fortress Press, 2010.

Kaiser, Walter C. Jr. *Toward an Exegetical Theology: Biblical Principals for Preaching and Teaching*. Grand Rapids: Baker Books Publishing. 1981.

Kennedy, George A. *New Testament Interpretation Through Rhetorical Criticism*. Chapel Hill: University of North Carolina Press. 1984.

Keefauver, Larry. *Smith Wigglesworth on Faith*. Mary: Charisma House Publishing. 1996.

Keener, Craig S. *The IVP Bible Background Commentary: New Testament*. Downers Grove: Intervarsity Press. 1993.

Ker, John. *The Psalms in History and Biography*. Eidenburgh: Andrew Elliot Printing. 1888.

Köstenberger, Andreas. Kellum, Scott L. Quarels, Charles L. *The Cradle the Cross and the Crown: An Introduction to the New Testament*. Nashville: B & H Academic Publishing. 2009.

_____. *Baker Exegetical Commentary on the New Testament. John*. Grand Rapids: Baker Academic Publishing. 2004.

Köstenberger, Andreas. *Excellence: The Character of God and the Pursuit of Scholarly Virtue*. Wheaton: Crossway Publishing. 2011.

Köstenberger, Andreas. Patterson, Richard D. *Invitation to Biblical Interpretation: Exploring the Hermeneutical Triad of History, Literature, and Theology*. Grand Rapids: Kregal Academic & Professional Publishing. 2011.

Lane, William L. *Word Biblical Commentary: Hebrews 1-8 vol. 47a*. Grand Rapids: Thomas Nelson Publishing. 1981.

Leifeld, Walter L. "Parables on Prayer" in *the Challenge of Jesus' Parables* ed. by Richard N. Longenecker. Grand Rapids: William B. Eerdmans Publishing. 2000.

Lewis, C.S. *Reflections on the Psalms*. New York: Harvest Book/Harcourt Publishing. 1958.

Longman, Tremper III. *Baker Commentary on the Old Testament Wisdom and Psalms*: Proverbs. Grand Rapids: Baker Academic Publishing. 2006.

BIBLIOGRAPHY

_____. *The New International Commentary on the Old Testament*, Ecclesiastes. Grand Rapids: William B. Eerdmans Publishing. 1998.

Longman, Tremper III, Dillard, Raymond B. *An Introduction to the Old Testament*: Second Edition. Grand Rapids: Zondervan Publishing. 1994.

Luther, Martin. *Luther's Small Catechism with Explanation*. St. Louis: Concordia Publishing House. 2005.

_____. *Prefaces to the New Testament*. St. Louis: Concordia Publishing House. 2010.

Malina, Bruce J. *Windows on the World of Jesus: Time Travel to Ancient Judea*. Louisville: Westminster John Knox Publishing. 1993.

Malina, Bruce J. and Richard Rohrbaugh. *Social Science Commentary on the Gospel of John*. Minneapolis: Fortress Press Publishing. 1998.

Marshal, I. Howard. *The New International Greek New Testament Commentary: Luke*. Grand Rapids: William B. Eerdmans Publishing. 1978.

McCann, J. Clinton. *New Interpreter's Bible, Psalms*, Vol. 4. Nashville: Abington Press. 1996.

McCartney, Dan. *Baker Exegetical Commentary*, James. Grand Rapids: Baker Books Publishing. 2009.

Merida, Tony, *Faithful Preaching: Declaring Scripture with Responsibility, Passion, and Authenticity*. Nashville: B&H Publishing, 2009.

Metzger, Bruce M. *Manuscripts of the Greek Bible: An Introduction to Greek Paleography*. Oxford: Oxford University Press. 1981.

Millard, Alan. *Reading and Writing in the Time of Jesus*, (New York: New York University Press, 2000).

Morris, Leon. *The New International Commentary on the New Testament. The Gospel According to John*. Revised Edition. Grand Rapids: William B. Eerdmans Publishing. 1995.

Mounce, William D. *Basics of Biblical Greek Grammar* 3rd ed. Grand Rapids: Zondervan Publishing. 2009.

O'Brien, Peter T. *Introductory Thanksgiving in the Letters of Paul*. Eugene: Wipf and Stock Publishing. 1977.

BIBLIOGRAPHY

_____. *The New International Greek Testament Commentary: The Epistle to the Philippians*. Grand Rapids: William B. Eerdmans Publishing. 1991.

_____. *Word Biblical Commentary: Colossians, Philemon*. Grand Rapids: Thomas Nelson Publishers. 1982.

Osborne, Grant R. *Exegetical Commentary on the New Testament: Matthew*. ed. Clinton C. Arnold. Grand Rapids: Zondervan Publishing. 2010.

_____. *The Hermeneutical Spiral: A Comprehensive Introduction to Biblical Interpretation*: revised and expanded edition. Downers Grove: IVP Press. 2006.

Packer, J.I. and Parrett Gary A. *Grounded in the Gospel: Building Believers the Old-Fashioned Way*. Grand Rapids: Baker Books Publishing. 2010.

Powell, Mark Allen. *What is Narrative Criticism?* Minneapolis: Augsburg Fortress Press. 1990.

Pratico, Gary D. Van Pelt, Miles V. *Basics of Biblical Hebrew Grammar*, Second Edition. Grand Rapids: Zondervan Publishing. 2007.

Price, Craig. *Biblical Exegesis of New Testament Greek*, James. Eugene: Cascade Books. 2008.

Rhoads, David. Dewey, Joanna. Michie, Donald. *Mark as Story: An Introduction to the Narrative of a Gospel*: 2nd ed. Minneapolis: Augsburg Fortress. 1999.

Richardson, Kurt A. *The New American Commentary*, James. Nashville: Broadman & Holman Publishers. 1997.

Ruskin, John. *Unto This Last and Other Writings*. London: Penguin Books Publishing. 1985.

Schweizer, Eduard. *The Good New According to Matthew*: trans. D.E. Green. Atlanta: John Knox Publishing. 1975.

Simmons, William A. *Peoples of the New Testament World: An Illustrated Guide*. Peabody: Hendrickson Publishing. 2008.

Snodgrass, Klyne R. *Stories with Intent: A Comprehensive Guide to the Parables of Jesus*. Grand Rapids: William B. Eerdmans Publishing. 2008.

Spatafora, Andrea. *From the Temple of God to God as the Temple: A Biblical Theological Study of the Temple in the Book of Revelation*. Rome: Gregorian University Press. 1997.

BIBLIOGRAPHY

Stevenson, Angus, Christine A Lindberg, ed. *New Oxford American Dictionary*, Third Edition. New York: Oxford University Press. 2010.

Suetonius. *The Twelve Caesars*. London: Penguin Books Publishing. 2003.

Sumney, Jerry L. *Philippians: A Greek Students Intermediate Reader*. Peabody: Hendrickson Publishing. 2007.

Talbert, Charles H. *Reading the Sermon on the Mount: Character Formation and Decision Making in Matthew 5-7*. Columbia: University of South Carolina Press. 2004.

Taylor, Bernard A. *Analytical Lexicon to the Septuagint*, Expanded Edition. Peabody: Hendrickson Publishing Marketing. 2009.

Thomas, Rosalind. *Literacy and Orality in Ancient Greece*, (Cambridge: Cambridge University Press, 1992).

Turner, David L. *Baker Exegetical Commentary on the New Testament: Matthew*. Grand Rapids: Baker Academic Publishing. 2008.

Vanhoozer, Kevin J. *The Drama of Doctrine: A Canonical Linguistic Approach to Christian Doctrine*. Louisville: Westminster John Knox Publishing. 2005.

Trenchard, Warren C. *Complete Vocabulary Guide to the Greek New Testament*. Grand Rapids: Zondervan Publishing. 1998.

Wallace, Daniel B. *Greek Grammar Beyond the Basics*. Grand Rapids: Zondervan Publishing. 1996.

Wells, David. *No Place for Truth or Whatever Happened to Evangelical Theology*. Grand Rapids: Eerdmans Publishing Company. 1993.

Wiarda, Timothy. *Interpreting Gospel Narratives: Scenes, People, and Theology*. Nashville: B & H Publishing. 2010.

Witherington, Ben III. *The Gospel of Mark: A Socio-Rhetorical Commentary*. Grand Rapids: William B. Eerdmans Publishing. 2001.

_____. *The Problem with Evangelical Theology: Testing the Exegetical Foundations of Calvinism, Dispensationalism, and Wesleyanism*. Waco: Baylor University Press. 2005.

BIBLIOGRAPHY

_____. *What Have They Done With Jesus? Beyond strange theories and bad history-Why we can trust the Bible.* New York: Harper SanFrancisco Publishing. 2006.

Young, C.D. *The Works of Philo: New Updated Version.* Peabody: Hendrickson Publishing. 2008.

Zacharias, Ravi. *Can Man Live Without God.* Nashville: W Publishing Group. 1994.

BIBLIOGRAPHY

Articles

Ahroni, Rueben "The Unity of Psalm 23" in the *Hebrew Annual Review* 6, 1982, p. 21-34.

Bovon, Francois. "The Parable of the Prodigal Son (Luke 15:11-32) First Reading" in Exegesis: Problems of Method and Exercises in Reading (Genesis 22 and Luke 15) ed. Franciois Bovon and Gregoire Rouiler; trans. Donald G. Miller, Pittsburgh; Pickwick, 1978, p. 43-73.

Cantwell, Laurence. "Immortal Longing in Sermone Humili: A Study of John 4:5-26" in the *Scottish Journal of Theology*, vol. 36. Issue 01, 1983. p. 73-86.

Charette, Blaine. "The Theme of Recompense in Matthew's Gospel" in the *Journal for the Study of the New Testament* Supplement Series 79. December 1992, 125.

Clines, D.J.A. "The Tree of Knowledge and the Law of Yahweh" in *Vetus Testamentum* 24, 1974, p. 8-14.

Cohick, Lynn H. "The Complete Work of Christ" in *Devotions on the Greek New Testament: 52 Reflections to Inspire & Instruct*, ed. J. Scott Duvall & Verlyn D. Verbrugge. Grand Rapids: Zondervan Publishing. 2012, p. 91-94.

Feldman, Louis H. "Financing the Colosseum" in Biblical Archaeology Review; Jul/Aug 2001, 27, p. 4.

Fredericks, D.C. "Qohelet's Language: Re-evaluating Its Nature and Date" in the *Ancient Near Eastern Texts*, 3rd edition. New York: Edwin Melen Publishing, 1988, p. 301.

Hendrickx, Herman. "'A Man Had Two Sons: Lk. 15:11-32' in Light of the Ancient Mediterranean Values of Farming and Househould.'" *East Asian Pastor Institute* 31, 1994, p.44-46.

Machen, J. Gresham The Minister and His Greek Testament, in the *Orthodox Presbyterian Church*, 1918.

Norris, Kathleen. "Incarnation Language" in *Christian Century* 114/22 (July 30 – August 6, 1997. p. 699.

Powell, Marvin A. "Weight and Measures" in the *Anchor Bible Dictionary*: vol. 6 ed. David Noel Freedman. New York: Doubleday Publishing. 1992, p. 897-908.

Smith, Argile. "Diminishing the Distance" in the *Theological Educator* No. 57, Spring 1998, p.121-8.

BIBLIOGRAPHY

Electronic Media

http://www.nttext.org/commentary

www.ingramcontent.com/pod-product-compliance
Lightning Source LLC
LaVergne TN
LVHW041541070426
835507LV00011B/855